the SECRET LIVES of BAKED GOODS

the SECRET LIVES of BAKED GOODS

Sweet Stories & Recipes for America's Favorite Desserts

JESSIE OLESON MOORE

Photographs by Clare Barboza

SASQUATCH BOOKS
SEATTLE

To Mom, Dad, Kelly, Bridget, and Porkchop for making life sweet

Copyright ©2013 by Jessie Oleson Moore

Printed in China

Published by Sasquatch Books
17 16 15 14 13   9 8 7 6 5 4 3 2 1

Editor: Susan Roxborough
Project editor: Michelle Hope Anderson
Design: Anna Goldstein
Illustrations: Jessie Oleson Moore
Photographs: Clare Barboza
Food styling: Laurie Pfalzer
Copy editor: Lisa Gordanier

Library of Congress Cataloging-in-Publication Data is available.

ISBN-13: 978-1-57061-853-6

Sasquatch Books
1904 Third Avenue, Suite 710
Seattle, WA 98101
(206) 467-4300
www.sasquatchbooks.com
custserv@sasquatchbooks.com

CONTENTS

ACKNOWLEDGMENTS

JUST AS MANY INGREDIENTS contribute to a recipe's deliciousness, many people contribute to baking up a book's successful completion! In the course of this project, I have many people to thank. Way too many for just one page, but I'll do the best I can.

Thank you to Sasquatch Books for believing in me enough to give me a second book deal. In particular, Susan Roxborough, Michelle Hope Anderson, and Anna Goldstein. For editing, photographing, and food styling, respectively: Lisa Gordanier, Clare Barboza, and Laurie Pfalzer. You all make me look (and sound) good!

Thanks to the ace group of testers and fact checkers for the recipes and stories in this book: Betsy Eves, Clara Nguyen Osborn, Jennifer Comfort, Jenny Williams, Tania Stenzel, Michelle Wall, Kristin Ausk, Nicole Vasquez, Porche Lovely, Compton Brodhead, Philip Longo. An extra-special thanks to Nancie and David Brodhead for the use of their kitchen for testing recipes!

Thanks to the companies and bakers whose recipes and stories inspired me. This book is my love letter to what you do and create!

For always supporting me, my family: Margie, Kenny, Kelly, Bridget, Dylan, and Porkchop. For always being my best friend: Danny Oleson. For always believing in me and always being willing to visit one more bakery: Becca Todd, Philip Longo, and James Papadopoulos.

And of course, all of the CakeSpy.com readers and enthusiasts. I love you to sugar-filled pieces.

And if you're just someone who thought the cover looked cool and picked up the book, well, thank you too for sharing a love of sweets. You're in for a real treat!

INTRODUCTION

*"Sometimes a person needs a story
more than food to stay alive."*

—BARRY LOPEZ, *CROW AND WEASEL*

HOW DO YOU INCREASE THE LURE OF DESSERT? With a little lore. I firmly believe that everything tastes better with a backstory; sweets, in particular, become far more pleasurable when served with a fascinating tale. Did you know, for instance, that chocolate chips were invented after the cookie? Chew on that: it will certainly make you taste your next cookie more mindfully.

Pausing to consider the stories of the treats we love gives us a chance to reflect on them and to appreciate the journeys they've taken to become part of our cookbook repertoire. It's also a chance to appreciate them anew.

One of the major lessons I've learned while writing this book is that recipes are not necessarily invented—they *evolve*. Much like playing the game Telephone, the stories of how they came to be can get a bit muddled with the passage of time. The recipes themselves, reflecting the tweaks that occur with repeated preparation, can change too—sometimes to the point where the dessert eventually bears little resemblance to the "original" version. While I've taken pains to find the true stories behind the sweets we love, sometimes determining the exact truth is not as much fun as examining the gossip surrounding them—so there's a bit of both here. I've researched, tested, and explored many versions of each recipe, both old and new (and had so much fun along the way!). I've striven to provide recipes that are respectful to the original, but updated, when appropriate, to make them more accessible to the home baker. In some cases, the recipes can be considered a starting place, an invitation for you, the baker, to add your own riffs and to weave your own stories into the results.

This book isn't intended as a textbook or a historical volume, but instead serves to tell stories and to celebrate sweets. Within these pages you'll find romantic musings on how confections got their names; stories of intrigue and even a bit of scandal; unusual facts and figures; and of course, many mouthwatering recipes and photos. Delightful and delicious, these tales are guaranteed to offer food for thought, and the recipes are bound to tantalize your sweet tooth.

CLASSIC CAKES

CAKES MAKE THE OCCASION. They're always the guest of honor, the prettiest food on the table, and (in my opinion) the most memorable part of a meal. They're a delicious symbol of celebration, and one of the sweetest food memories we hold onto. Here's a collection of classics, each served with a sweet story.

Birthday Cake

WHEN YOU THINK ABOUT IT, birthday cake is kind of a funny thing: what other dessert do you put candles on, sing to, spit at as you try to blow out the candles, and then watch as your friends and family clamor for a piece? And yet, birthday cake is one of the most popular desserts in America. Everyone can picture the classic two-layer round cake, filled and covered with a thick layer of fluffy frosting, topped (if you're lucky) with bright decorations, and finished with a blaze of candles on top. But how on earth did this dessert become the symbol of celebrating another year of life?

. . . .

The idea of punctuating special occasions with cake is nothing new. Putting together all of the richest and best ingredients for celebrations was common even in ancient times. In days past, however, special-occasion cakes probably resembled fruitcakes more than the fluffy layer cakes we know and love today.

What happened to take us from eating leaden fruitcakes to blowing out candles atop sprinkle-festooned cakes? That would have been a little something called the Industrial Revolution, which resulted in better transportation, improved production methods, and unbelievable innovation. The pleasant side effects for the world of commercial and home baking were the dropping costs of sugar, butter, spices, and flour; the invention of baking powder; and the development of better ovens. Baking suddenly became a piece of . . . well, you know. Due to a more convenient lifestyle, "regular people" had more time to entertain—and that meant baking up something special for dessert. Suddenly, there was a new generation of frequent cake eaters who expected to be wowed on their birthdays.

But without candles, it's just cake, right? Some say the ancient Greeks placed lit candles on cakes to make them glow "like the moon," so the smoke would carry their prayers to the gods. The art of the birthday candle was further developed

In days past, special-occasion cakes probably resembled fruitcakes more than the fluffy layer cakes we know and love today.

in Germany, where candles corresponding to age were placed on cakes, along with one in the center "to grow on." Today, the custom involves making a silent wish when the candles are blown out; the belief is that blowing out all the candles in one breath means the wish will come true and the person will enjoy good luck in the coming year.

Even after this sweet backstory, you may still find yourself wondering, "What flavor *is* a birthday cake, exactly?" The answer: Whatever you want it to be. In the past, all celebration cakes might have had the same basic ingredients—the expensive stuff, like nuts and fruits—but today we bake birthday cakes to reflect the wishes or the personality of the birthday boy or girl. For older celebrants, it's often a nostalgic treat reminiscent of what they enjoyed when they were kids.

So whether it's a banana cake with cream cheese frosting, a chocolate torte, or even a fanciful cake decorated to look like a dragon, it's all right. I've chosen to celebrate the iconic American birthday cake with a recipe that will never go out of style: buttery yellow cake with fudgy chocolate frosting and hopefully some sprinkles—a perfect way to celebrate your special day.

Yellow Birthday Cake

THIS DELICIOUS CAKE IS RICH WITH egg yolks, sour cream, and butter (it's OK—you deserve it). If you want to make the cake layers ahead so you have time to concentrate on blowing up balloons, go ahead and bake them, wrap them well, and freeze them for up to a week in advance. Thaw the cakes (still wrapped) before assembling with an abundance of chocolate frosting.

Makes one 8- or 9-inch layer cake (10 to 12 servings)

1. Preheat the oven to 350 degrees F. Grease and flour two 8- or 9-inch round baking pans, then line them with circles of parchment paper.

2. Sift together the flour, baking powder, and salt; set aside.

3. In the bowl of a stand mixer fitted with the paddle attachment, cream the butter on medium speed for about 2 minutes, scraping the bowl as needed. Add the sugars and continue to mix until light and fluffy, another 2 to 3 minutes.

4. Add the egg yolks one at a time, ensuring that each is incorporated before adding the next. Stir in the vanilla.

5. Reduce the mixer speed to low and add the dry ingredients alternately with the sour cream, in 2 to 3 additions each, ensuring that each addition is fully incorporated before adding the next. Stir in the milk. Scrape down the sides of the bowl with a rubber spatula after each addition.

6. In a separate bowl, making sure that the bowl and beaters are very clean (so that the egg whites will whip properly), beat the egg whites to soft peaks. Gently fold the whipped egg whites into the batter, using a rubber spatula.

7. Pour the batter into the prepared pans and smooth with an offset or rubber spatula. Bake for 35 to 45 minutes, or until the cakes are golden brown on top and a toothpick inserted into the center of the cake comes out clean.

8. Let the cakes cool in the pans for 5 minutes; run a paring knife around the perimeter of the cakes to release any sticky parts, then

2¼ cups sifted cake flour

2 teaspoons baking powder

½ teaspoon salt

1 cup (2 sticks) unsalted butter, softened

1½ cup granulated sugar

¼ cup packed light brown sugar

4 large eggs, separated

2 teaspoons vanilla extract

1 cup sour cream

¼ cup whole or 2% milk

3½ cups Rich Chocolate Frosting (recipe follows)

Decorating icing, sprinkles, or other decorations (optional)

turn them out onto a wire rack. Let the cakes cool completely. If the cakes are domed on top, use a serrated knife to make them level.

9. To assemble, place one cake layer, bottom side up, on a serving platter, and spread ½ to ¾ cup frosting on top. Leave a ½-inch margin all around, as the weight of the second cake layer will push the frosting to the edges. Place the second cake layer, flat side up, on top of the frosted layer. Frost the sides and top, and garnish with decorating icing, sprinkles, or whatever festive treats you'd like. Store, well covered, at cool room temperature for up to 2 days (although, who has leftover birthday cake?).

RICH CHOCOLATE FROSTING

Makes about 3½ cups frosting

1 cup (2 sticks) unsalted butter, softened

½ teaspoon salt

2 teaspoons vanilla extract

3 to 4 cups confectioners' sugar

½ cup unsweetened cocoa powder

¼ cup heavy cream

1. In a stand mixer fitted with the paddle attachment, cream the butter on high speed until smooth, about 1 minute. Stir in the salt and vanilla.

2. In a separate bowl, sift together 3 cups of the sugar with the cocoa.

3. Add the sugar mixture to the butter mixture in 2 to 3 additions, beating on low speed. Pause to scrape down the sides of the bowl with a rubber spatula after each addition.

4. Add the cream; increase the speed to medium, and beat until the mixture is very fluffy. Add the remaining sugar incrementally until it has reached your desired spreading consistency.

Boston Cream Pie

HERE'S A PIE THAT IS LIVING A LIE: It's actually a cake. Certainly it has no reason to hide its true identity: it's a respectable cake indeed—sort of an expanded version of an éclair, comprised of light-yet-buttery spongy layers and an amazingly addictive cream filling that makes you wonder how quickly you could eat your weight in it. But wait, there's more: it's topped with a rich chocolate glaze.

. . . .

When it comes to its pedigree, this cake is the result of beautiful fusion: it was inspired by English cakes, and invented by an Armenian-French pastry chef who lived in America. His name was M. Sanzian (nobody even knows what his first name was), and it all went down at the Parker House Hotel in the 1850s. The Parker House PR department says that the hotel's concept of providing its clientele with extremely elegant lodgings stretched to its cuisine. During a time when a good cook could be hired for $416 a year, the Parker House hired M. Sanzian for an unheard-of salary of $5,000 per year. That's a lot of dough.

Dedicating such a lavish salary wasn't out of character for this hotel, which prided itself on being a groundbreaker. Among other things, it was the first hotel in Boston to have hot and cold running water, and the first to have an elevator. It was known to attract famous guests, including Charles Dickens, Henry Wadsworth Longfellow, and actress Sarah Bernhard (who also has a cake named after her). Lemon meringue pie (page 75) is also cited as a sweet that was perfected and popularized in the Parker House kitchens. And certainly having the mystery French chef invent Boston cream pie, the now iconic American dessert, is another feather in their already well-adorned cap.

In 1996, it became the official state dessert of Massachusetts, thanks to the lobbying work of a dedicated high school civics class.

While this may explain how the influential hotel popularized the dessert, it doesn't quite explain the sticky subject of why it was called a pie. Happily, there are some respectable theories. At the time it was invented, pie tins were much more common in American households than cake pans as we know them now—so perhaps cakes and pies were interchangeable in that way. A look at a cookbook of the era shows that while Washington pie and Boston cream pie were both labeled as "pies," the instructions reference "the cake." Or perhaps it has something to do with the fact that a French pastry chef living in America invented it; this new invention was certainly different from the multi-layered gateaux and fancy pastries he was accustomed to, perhaps confusing the classification of this cake.

But what really made Boston cream pie revolutionary, claims the book *You Know You're in Massachusetts When . . .* , is the use of a chocolate topping "in an era when chocolate was primarily used at home, and then for beverages and puddings, not as an ingredient in restaurant pastries." It goes on to say that "with the increasing popularity of chocolate in the 20th century, the Boston cream pie became a staple of American kitchens. Betty Crocker even offered it as a mix from 1958 into the 1990s."

In 1996, it became the official state dessert of Massachusetts, thanks to the lobbying work of a dedicated high school civics class. The pie beat out some other pretty powerhouse candidates, including the Toll House Cookie and Indian Pudding. But all rivalries are put aside and everyone is a Bostonian on October 23rd, which is—as I'm sure you know—National Boston Cream Pie Day!

The following recipe uses a chocolate ganache glaze instead of the original chocolate fondant—trust me, unless you happen to own a marble slab and enjoy the hours-long production of creating the original, you're really better off this way. If you want to explore another flavor variation on this treat, omit the chocolate and insert a layer of raspberry jam between the cake layers—it's then called Washington pie, another recipe that enjoyed popularity in the 1800s.

Boston Cream Pie

YOU MIGHT THINK THAT THE AMOUNT OF PASTRY CREAM in this recipe is excessive, but once spread lusciously between the layers, it makes sense. This recipe is adapted from the version served at Boston's Omni Parker House Hotel, but made a little, well, easier for the home cook.

Makes one 10-inch layer cake (10 to 12 servings)

7 large eggs

1 cup sugar, divided

1 cup all-purpose flour

2 tablespoons butter, melted

5 cups Pastry Cream (recipe follows)

1¾ cups Rich Chocolate Topping (recipe follows)

½ cup sliced almonds

1. Preheat the oven to 350 degrees F. Grease and flour the bottom and sides of a 10-inch springform pan.

2. Carefully separate the eggs, putting the whites and the yolks in separate large bowls; make sure there are no specks of yolk in the egg whites (the whites won't whip properly if there are). Add ½ cup of the sugar to each bowl.

3. In the bowl of an electric mixer fitted with the whisk attachment, beat the egg whites on medium-high speed until they form stiff peaks; set aside. Using an electric mixer or by hand, beat the egg yolks until they are thick and pale yellow in color. Stir about one-quarter of the whites in to the yolks to lighten the batter, then gently fold the rest of the whites into the yolk mixture.

4. Whisk the flour into the egg mixture using a large balloon-type whisk, working carefully to minimize the deflation of the batter. Then, using the same whisk, stir in the melted butter. Pour the batter into the prepared cake pan, filling it about three-quarters of the way, and bake for 15 to 20 minutes, or until a toothpick inserted into the center of the cake comes out clean. Let the cake cool in the pan for about 30 minutes, then remove it from the pan and transfer to a wire rack to cool completely.

5. To assemble the cake, using a long serrated knife, slice the cake horizontally into 2 equal layers. Place one of the cake layers, cut side up, on a sheet of parchment paper (this will catch any drips, and allow easy cleanup before transferring it to a serving platter). Spoon the pastry cream onto the center of the bottom layer, leaving 1½ inches uncovered on all sides—the weight of the top cake layer will spread it to the edges. You will not need all of the pastry cream; reserve a small quantity to spread around the sides of the cake.

6. Place the second layer of cake on top of the pastry cream, then spread the remaining pastry cream around the sides of the cake. Using a ladle, spoon the still slightly warm chocolate glaze on the top of the cake, allowing it to gently drip over the sides. Gently press the almonds around the sides or on the top. Serve immediately at room temperature, or refrigerate for up to 2 days, well wrapped, and bring to a cool room temperature before serving.

PASTRY CREAM

Makes about 5 cups cream

2 tablespoon butter
1½ cups whole or 2% milk
2½ cups heavy cream
½ cup sugar
3 tablespoons cornstarch
6 large eggs

1. In a medium saucepan over medium-high heat, combine the butter, milk, and cream. Bring to a simmer, then remove from heat.

2. In a large bowl, whisk the sugar and cornstarch until combined. Add the eggs, beating until the mixture is light yellow and forms ribbons when you lift the whisk, about 5 minutes by hand.

3. Slowly pour the milk mixture into the egg mixture, whisking until completely combined.

4. Pour into a medium pot and place over medium heat. Heat, whisking constantly to keep the eggs from cooking. The mixture will begin to bubble. Continue whisking until the mixture has thickened to the consistency of a pudding; this will happen about 2 minutes after it comes to a boil. If any bits of egg have cooked, forming lumps, strain the mixture through a mesh sieve.

5. Transfer to a bowl and press plastic wrap directly onto the surface of the custard to keep a skin from forming. Refrigerate for several hours, or until completely chilled.

RICH CHOCOLATE TOPPING

Makes about 1¾ cups glaze

1 cup heavy cream
8 ounces semisweet chocolate, finely chopped (about 1 cup)

1. In a medium saucepan over medium heat, bring the cream to a boil. Place the chocolate in a medium bowl; pour the hot cream over the chocolate, stirring until the chocolate is melted and the mixture is well combined. Set aside to cool slightly, about 10 minutes.

THE FICTIONAL BALLAD OF BETTY AND DUNCAN

SOMETIMES, WHEN I'M BEING PARTICULARLY INVENTIVE in the kitchen, I think of myself as the forbidden love child of Betty Crocker and Duncan Hines. But did Betty and Duncan really exist?

Duncan Hines, the brand, is based on a real person. An insurance man who was frequently on the road, Hines began documenting the restaurants he enjoyed on his business trips. He distributed this list at first as a favor to friends, but his guide was soon being requested beyond that circle, and before you knew it, his volumes were published. The Duncan Hines Seal of Approval became a trusted mark of quality, allowing individuals and families to try out establishments with confidence. Hines's career later shifted to that of the pre–Food Network foodie: he wrote guides and had a column in the newspaper. His respected name attracted a licensing deal to put it on a number of food products. The cake mixes in particular succeeded, and they have become the lasting legacy of Duncan Hines.

But as for Betty—well, she's *really* not real. She was—and still is—a benevolent marketing tool of General Mills, Inc., invented to respond to customer inquiries about baking when the volume became too great for the company's male CEO to respond to (it's also said that his comfort level at answering ladies' inquiries was not especially high). Betty Crocker grew beyond a mere personality to become a beloved baking confidante: her star rose through her presence in magazine advertisements, newspaper columns, and most notably, through a popular radio program. Actresses would play the role of Betty, whose voice and likeness became a friendly, trusted voice to the American housewife.

Not everyone was aware that Betty's was a collective voice, however: when General Mills began offering tours of the Betty Crocker test kitchens, it came to the point where they'd have to keep tissues on hand for visitors who found out—their dreams dashed—that they wouldn't get to meet Betty herself at the end of the tour.

While General Mills has never exactly kept these details a secret, it's still a popular belief that Betty is (or at least was) a real person. Talk about batter banter for your next party!

Carrot Cake

ALTHOUGH IT WOULD BE A STRETCH to call this homespun favorite a high-stylin' dessert, carrot cake—a lumpy and slightly frumpy but incredibly moist and flavorful carrot-flecked spice cake—has enjoyed several moments in vogue over the years.

. . . .

The use of carrots in desserts actually dates back to medieval times, when carrot pudding was enjoyed as a sweet treat at banquets. This was probably borne out of necessity, making use of the carrots' natural sweetness (they contain more sugar than any other vegetable besides the sugar beet); while the pudding would have been steamed and vaguely cakelike, it didn't bear much resemblance to our modern carrot cake. Because as much as you search for it, you're not going to find any mention of a recipe for medieval cream cheese frosting.

A big development in the world of carrot cake came in the early 1900s, when carrot pudding began to be baked in loaf pans, more like a quick bread. By mid-century, the carrot cake had hopped over to America, where it would make dessert history. There's a delightful story indicating that there was a glut of canned carrots in the United States. An enterprising businessman named George C. Page hired bakers to find uses for the excess; they settled on carrot cake, which Page then sold through the company Mission Pak, a large purveyor of gourmet foods.

Of course, the thing that really separates carrot cake from being equivalent to eating a salad is the thick slather of cream cheese, butter, and sugar that became the frosting of choice in the 1960s.

Of course, the thing that really separates carrot cake from being equivalent to eating a salad is the thick slather of cream cheese, butter, and sugar that became the frosting of choice in the 1960s, a time during which Philadelphia

Cream Cheese appeared on every grocery store shelf, everywhere. It's possible this is when carrot cake and cream cheese frosting really became a bonded pair, maintaining a sort of common-law marriage that is still kicking today.

If you're a baby-boomer-former-hippie (or the offspring of one), you'll remember that carrot cake really caught on in a big way in the health-conscious 1970s, when it was touted as being "healthy." And really, the idea isn't too far-flung: after all, carrots are vegetables, and raisins and nuts *are* pretty much health food, right?

Carrot cake can feature a variety of fun and tasty additions, and those can be the subject of some argument. No matter what, carrot cake's mild but distinct flavor, with its pretty little flecks of orange, have made the cake an enduring favorite. While few would think of it as haute couture, it's considered a time-less classic that never goes out of style.

Carrot Cake

I'VE KEPT THINGS PRETTY SIMPLE in this recipe so that you can choose your own add-ins. While raisins are the most common complement to carrots in this cake, many modern palates prefer pineapple, coconut, apples, or applesauce; sometimes walnuts, sometimes pecans, sometimes no nuts at all. So feel free to tailor the cake to your liking—and if you want to think of it as health food, go ahead—I won't stop you.

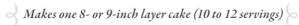

Makes one 8- or 9-inch layer cake (10 to 12 servings)

1. Preheat the oven to 350 degrees F. Grease and flour 2 round 8- or 9-inch cake pans; line the bottoms of the pans with parchment paper.

2. In a medium bowl, sift together the flour, baking soda, baking powder, salt, and cinnamon. Set aside.

3. In the bowl of a stand mixer fitted with the paddle attachment, combine the eggs, oil, sugars, and vanilla. Beat on low speed for about 30 seconds, then increase the speed to medium and beat for about 3 minutes, or until well combined and lightly frothy.

4. Reduce the speed to low and add the flour mixture in 2 to 3 increments, pausing to scrape down the sides of the bowl with a rubber spatula after each addition. Add the carrots, mixing until combined. Fold in the 1 cup pecans. Divide the batter evenly between each of the prepared pans.

5. Bake for 35 to 45 minutes, or until a toothpick inserted into the center of the cakes comes out clean. Let the cakes cool in the pan for 10 minutes, run a paring knife around the perimeter of the cakes to release any sticky parts, then turn out onto a wire rack. Peel off the parchment paper and allow the cakes to cool completely before frosting them.

6. Once cooled, place one cake layer, flat side up, on a serving platter; spread ¾ to 1 cup of frosting on top. Leave a ½-inch margin all around, as the weight of the second cake layer will push the frosting to the edges. Place the second cake layer, flat side up, on top of the

2 cups all-purpose flour

2 teaspoons baking soda

2 teaspoons baking powder

½ teaspoon salt

2 teaspoons ground cinnamon

4 large eggs

1¼ cups vegetable oil

1 cup granulated sugar

1 cup packed light brown sugar

2 teaspoons vanilla extract

3 cups lightly packed grated carrots (4 to 5 medium carrots)

1 cup chopped toasted pecans, plus ½ cup toasted pecan halves, for garnish

3 cups Cream Cheese Frosting (recipe follows)

frosted layer. Spread the remainder of the frosting on the sides and top. Garnish with the pecan halves.

7. Serve at room temperature. Because the cream cheese frosting is sensitive to heat, store lightly covered in the refrigerator for up to 3 days; let come to room temperature before serving.

CREAM CHEESE FROSTING

Makes about 3 cups frosting

8 ounces (1 cup) cream cheese, softened

½ cup (1 stick) butter, softened

1 teaspoon vanilla extract

½ teaspoon salt

4 to 5 cups confectioners' sugar, sifted

1. In the bowl of a stand mixer fitted with the paddle attachment, combine the cream cheese, butter, vanilla, and salt. Beat at medium-high speed until the mixture has a very smooth consistency; pause to scrape down the bowl with a rubber spatula as needed. Add the confectioners' sugar 1 cup at a time, mixing after each addition, until the frosting is smooth and spreadable.

Cupcakes

THERE'S A LOT TO LOVE ABOUT CUPCAKES. They've got a fantastic ratio of cake (little) to frosting (lots), they're cute as a button, and they induce a sweet nostalgia that is practically guaranteed to take you back—just for a moment—to your sixth birthday party. These days, they're readily available in a dizzying array of colors and flavors at cupcake-specific boutiques known as "cupcakeries." But how did these miniature cakes come to be so popular?

. . . .

The idea of baking cakes in smaller portions has existed for quite some time. In *American Cookery* by Amelia Simmons (the hottest recipe book around in 1796), a recipe calls for cakes to be "baked in small cups." The actual term "cupcake" appeared not long after, in another early American cookbook, *Seventy-Five Receipts for Pastry, Cakes and Sweetmeats* by Eliza Leslie.

One reason that baking cakes in smaller portions became popular is a practical one: they bake quicker than large cakes, which—if you were the one stoking that wood-fired cast-iron oven—was a definite plus. Bakers used pans called gem pans, a pretty name for a clunky pan: large, heavy, usually cast-iron precursors to today's muffin tins, they were a common household item in the early 1900s. Paper baking cups first came about following World War II, when an artillery manufacturer began to make paper baking products as the need for weapons declined. Within a few decades, the liners had gained popularity with home bakers, making for a quick clean-up.

The first truly famous cupcake, the chocolate Hostess snack cupcake, was introduced in the early 1900s. Early versions were hand-frosted, but lacked the signature loop-de-loop decoration and cream filling; those wonderful traits didn't come until the middle of the century, when manufacturing innovations made it possible. Throughout the 1900s, cupcakes became an increasingly

Cupcakes are an affordable luxury; they're cute and nostalgic; and best of all, it's socially acceptable not to share.

popular kids' treat. I can certainly attest to why baking cupcakes caught on big at *my* house. If you tried to sneak a taste of mom's layer cake before dessert, you would *definitely* be caught. But chances were, you could snag an entire cupcake and not get busted like a buttercream bandit.

Given their popularity, it would be hard to say that cupcakes were ever *out*, but it's certain that by the 1990s, they became decidedly *in*. Bakeries in New York City, such as Magnolia Bakery and the Cupcake Café, pioneered boutique cupcakeries. The concept captured the imagination of the public, and before you knew it, at Magnolia Bakery in particular, there were lines around the block of eager eaters waiting for a cupcake fix. As a result, a cupcake shop revolution was born—today, there's at least one, if not ten or twenty, in every major city.

While this causes battle cries of "Cupcakes are so over!" by sophisticated foodies who bemoan the cutesy cupcake trend, the shops continue to flourish, and with good reason. Cupcakes are an affordable luxury; they're cute and nostalgic; and best of all, it's socially acceptable not to share. Finally, decorating them is an art in itself, with creative shop owners and home bakers whipping up beautiful, whimsical, and sometimes awe-inspiring designs.

Coconut Cupcakes

IN AMERICA'S SOUTHERN STATES, coconut cake is considered a "legacy cake," meaning that it has cultural and historical significance and is especially beloved by the local populace. It's always a crowd pleaser and is a very pretty dessert to serve, with its shaggy, confetti-like finished look. It's especially adorable in cupcake form! You can personalize the li'l cakes for an event by tinting the coconut and the frosting to suit the occasion.

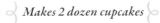 *Makes 2 dozen cupcakes*

1. Preheat the oven to 350 degrees F. Line two 12-cup muffin tins with cupcake papers.

2. Mix the flour, baking powder, baking soda, and salt in a medium bowl; set aside.

3. In the bowl of a stand mixer fitted with the paddle attachment, cream the butter and sugar until light and fluffy, 3 to 5 minutes. Add the eggs, one at a time, beating well after each addition; scrape down the bowl with a rubber spatula as needed. Beat in the extracts.

4. Add the flour mixture to the egg mixture in 2 or 3 additions, alternately with the milk, beating well after each addition. Fold in 1 cup of the coconut by hand.

5. Fill the lined muffin cups two-thirds of the way full. Bake for 18 to 20 minutes, or until a toothpick inserted into the center comes out clean. Transfer the pans to wire racks to cool completely.

6. Frost the cooled cupcakes. Use the remaining 2 cups coconut as is (alternatively, toast in the oven at 300 degrees F until golden brown, and let cool, or tint it using food coloring), placing it in a bowl and turning cupcakes, frosting side down, into the coconut, coating generously.

3 cups all-purpose flour

1 teaspoon baking powder

½ teaspoon baking soda

½ teaspoon salt

1½ cups (3 sticks) unsalted butter, softened

1¾ cups sugar

5 large eggs

1 teaspoon vanilla extract

1 teaspoon coconut extract (or 1 extra teaspoon of vanilla extract)

1 cup whole or 2% milk

1 cup sweetened flaked coconut

3 cups Coconut Cream Frosting (recipe follows)

2 cups sweetened flaked coconut, for garnish

COCONUT CREAM FROSTING

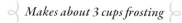

Makes about 3 cups frosting

1. In a stand mixer fitted with the paddle attachment, beat the butter, salt, and coconut extract until smooth. On low speed, gradually beat in the confectioners' sugar 1 cup at a time, until your desired consistency has been reached. If the mixture becomes too thick, thin it with the cream or milk. Cover the frosting tightly and keep it chilled until you're ready to frost the cupcakes.

1 cup (2 sticks) unsalted butter, softened

¼ teaspoon salt

1 teaspoon coconut extract

4 to 5 cups confectioners' sugar

2 to 3 tablespoons heavy cream or milk (optional)

German Chocolate Cake

THIS CAKE IS NAMED AFTER A GERMAN, but not the Teutonic type. It bears the name of a man called Samuel German, whose Baker's German's Sweet Chocolate was the base for this American classic: multiple layers (usually three) of airy-but-rich chocolate cake filled and then topped off with a spectacular slurry of buttery brown sugar, toasty coconut, and pecans. It's a pity, though, that German never got to taste the cake that bears his name.

. . . .

Without Baker's chocolate there would be no cake, so first let me tell you a little about the company. The business began in 1765, when Dr. James Baker and a partner went into the chocolate-making business to capitalize on chocolate's growing popularity in the colonies. When the Revolution broke out and importing became decidedly more difficult, the company smuggled shipments of cacao beans on Royal Navy warships in order to continue production (although there is no documentation regarding whether or not the forbidden chocolate tasted better than its lawful counterpart). After Baker's partner failed to return from a chocolate mission to the West Indies, he formed Baker's Chocolate Company, which has been in business since 1780—making it America's oldest chocolate company.

As the business grew, so did its product offerings. In 1852, employee Samuel German invented a new type of sweet baking chocolate, which was named in his honor. Its unique blend was sweeter than semisweet or bittersweet baking chocolate, and it was considered easier on the palate. In retrospect, this sweet baking chocolate was a precursor to milk chocolate, which would gain popularity later on in the century.

But oh, if German could have seen what happened a hundred years later.

In 1957, a recipe titled German's Chocolate Cake was sent by a Dallas, Texas, homemaker to a local newspaper. Her recipe used German's chocolate, at the time a somewhat obscure ingredient. But it certainly appealed to readers' taste buds—today, we might say this recipe "went viral." Requests started streaming in to General Foods, who had acquired Baker's, about how to obtain the chocolate; they took note and marketed the recipe to newspapers all around the country. Sales of Baker's chocolate increased dramatically.

Her recipe used German's chocolate, at the time a somewhat obscure ingredient. But it certainly appealed to readers' taste buds—today, we might say this recipe "went viral."

As for "German"? The possessive form (German's) was dropped somewhere along the line, making for the German chocolate cake name we know today.

German Chocolate Cake

THIS RECIPE IS QUITE TRUE TO EARLY VERSIONS, with chocolate cake layers and a sticky, addictive pecan-coconut-caramel filling. It's not necessarily a sophisticated-looking dessert, but it makes for some seriously sweet homespun eating. And while, of course, I recommend using the original Baker's chocolate for this recipe, you can use any chocolate with a cacao content of less than 50 percent.

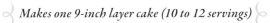

Makes one 9-inch layer cake (10 to 12 servings)

2 ¼ cups cake flour

1 teaspoon baking soda

½ teaspoon salt

4 ounces sweet baking chocolate (preferably Baker's German), chopped (about ½ cup)

½ cup water

4 eggs, separated

1 cup (2 sticks) unsalted butter, softened

2 cups sugar

2 teaspoons vanilla extract

1 cup buttermilk

4 cups Coconut Pecan Frosting (recipe follows)

3 tablespoons Chocolate Drizzle (recipe follows)

1. Position a rack in the center of the oven; preheat the oven to 350 degrees F. Grease and flour the sides and bottoms of 3 round 9-inch cake pans; line the bottoms of the pans with parchment paper.

2. Sift the flour, baking soda, and salt in a large bowl. Set aside.

3. In a double boiler, warm the chocolate and water over medium-low heat until the chocolate has melted, stirring to combine. Remove from heat and set aside.

4. Using the clean, dry bowl of a stand mixer fitted with the whisk attachment, or in a medium bowl with a hand mixer, whip the egg whites on high speed until stiff peaks form; set aside.

5. In a stand mixer fitted with the paddle attachment, cream the butter and sugar on medium speed until light and fluffy, 3 to 5 minutes. Add the egg yolks one at a time, beating well after each addition; pause to scrape down the sides of the bowl with a rubber spatula as needed. Blend in the chocolate mixture and the vanilla. Add the flour mixture alternately with the buttermilk in 2 or 3 additions, beating until well blended after each addition.

6. Fold the beaten egg whites into the mixture by hand until well blended. Divide the batter evenly between the 3 pans, smoothing and leveling the tops with a rubber or offset spatula.

7. Bake for 26 to 30 minutes, or until a toothpick inserted into the center of the cakes comes out mostly clean.

8. Cool the cakes in the pans for about 20 minutes, then invert them onto wire racks to cool completely.

9. To assemble the cake, set one of the layers on a plate flat side up. Spread one-third of the frosting on top, stopping a little short of the outside edges of the cake. Add another cake layer, press lightly, and repeat. Place your last cake on top and spread the remainder of the frosting over the top. The sides of the cake will remain exposed.

10. Drizzle the glaze down the sides of the cake.

11. This cake will keep, lightly covered at cool room temperature, for up to 4 days.

COCONUT PECAN FROSTING

 Makes about 4 cups frosting

1. Combine the sugar, evaporated milk, butter, and egg yolks in a large saucepan. Cook over low heat, whisking frequently, until the mixture begins bubbling; increase the heat to medium and continue whisking constantly until the mixture has thickened and turned golden in color. This can take about 10 to 15 minutes. Remove from heat. Stir in coconut, pecans, and vanilla. Cool to lukewarm, or until thick enough to spread.

2 cups sugar

2 cups evaporated milk

1 cup (2 sticks) butter

6 egg yolks, lightly beaten

2¾ cups sweetened flaked coconut

2 cups chopped toasted pecans

1½ teaspoons vanilla extract

CHOCOLATE DRIZZLE

 Makes 3 tablespoons drizzle

1. In a small saucepan, melt the butter and chocolate. Stir until smooth.

½ teaspoon unsalted butter

1 ounce semisweet chocolate

New York Cheesecake

IN SPITE OF WHAT NEW YORKERS may have you believe, they did not invent cheesecake—it's actually been around since ancient Roman times. In Italy, the cake is coarser and less sweet, usually made with ricotta cheese; some versions are even savory. But New York was the melting pot in which this cake was adopted, wrapped in a cream cheese–coated bear hug, and transformed into the remarkably dense, sweet, creamy dessert we know today. To put it in simpler terms, "Cheesecake wasn't really cheesecake till it was cheesecake in New York."

. . . .

Oddly enough, the thing that the Empire State *can* legitimately claim credit for is cream cheese—but ironically, the first (and arguably still most famous) brand, Philadelphia Cream Cheese, takes its name from a city miles away. Cream cheese was invented by accident in 1872 by William Lawrence of Chester, New York, while he was trying to reproduce a French cheese called Neufchâtel (which, interestingly, is now often marketed as low-fat cream cheese). Under the name Empire Company, Lawrence distributed this cheese in distinctive foil wrappers; and in the 1880s, the name was changed to Philadelphia Brand Cream Cheese—still the brand favored by many home bakers today.

It's hard to know who first substituted cream cheese for ricotta in an Italian cheesecake recipe. But New York–style cheesecake became famous in the 1920s when it was featured by popular Jewish delicatessens—notably Lindy's in Manhattan and Junior's in Brooklyn. The smooth texture of the cream cheese paired with a sweeter filling and crust made it a new thing entirely.

New York was the melting pot in which this cake was adopted, wrapped in a cream cheese–coated bear hug, and transformed into the remarkably dense, sweet, creamy dessert we know today.

Its popularity spread, and soon it became a highly sought-after item on dessert carts around the country.

As for the graham cracker crust that has become so popular with New York–style cheesecake? It's not a vital part of the earliest recipes, many of which feature a more cake-like cookie crust, but it quickly caught on—who can resist the crunch of the cracker against the creaminess of the cheese filling? Its popularity spiked following a series of promotional recipes created by Nabisco that appeared in advertisements and on packaging.

To summarize: No, the cheesecake was not invented in New York City. But that "dear old dirty town" has done a fantastic job of raising the bar and making it into something great. A fat slice of silky-smooth cheesecake is often seen as the most decadent dessert of all: ultimately craveable, it's the downfall of many a diet. Like the city it calls home, this cake is a big, assertive, and unapologetic salute to excess.

New York Cheesecake

EVEN A VERY DENSE CHEESECAKE like this can be somewhat fragile, so be sure to allow plenty of time for baking, cooling, and then thoroughly chilling it. As for serving the dessert, a few small tips may help: slice it by using dental floss (unflavored) rather than a knife, which will immediately create a bit of a mess. And if cracks appear on the surface, do not panic; when in doubt, top it with cherries, strawberries, and whipped or sour cream. This recipe is adapted from the one famously served at Lindy's in New York City.

 *Makes one 9-inch cheesecake (10 servings)*

2½ pounds (five 8-ounce packages) full-fat cream cheese, softened

1¾ cups sugar

2 teaspoons grated lemon zest

1 teaspoon vanilla extract

5 large eggs, plus 2 yolks, at room temperature

¼ cup heavy cream

Shortcrust Cheesecake Base (recipe follows)

1. Line the bottom of a 9-by-4-inch springform pan with a circle of parchment paper; grease the bottom and sides.

2. Preheat the oven to 500 degrees F.

3. In a stand mixer fitted with the paddle attachment, mix the cream cheese at medium speed until it is extremely smooth; this will take several minutes.

4. Add the sugar in 2 additions, pausing to scrape down the sides of the bowl with a rubber spatula with each addition. Mix in the lemon zest and vanilla.

5. Add the eggs, one at a time, with the 2 extra yolks added last, pausing after each addition to scrape down the sides of the bowl. Add the cream, mixing until smooth. When completely smooth and creamy, the filling is ready to be poured into the crust.

6. To bake the cheesecake, pour the cheesecake mixture into the prebaked crust and bake for 10 minutes; reduce the heat to 250 degrees F, and bake for 55 to 60 minutes, or until the top is golden. The center will still appear to be somewhat wobbly; as the cake cools, it will set. Cool completely before cutting, about 3 hours in the refrigerator. To store, wrap the cheesecake well and refrigerate for up to 4 days.

SHORTCRUST CHEESECAKE BASE

 Makes one 9-by-4-inch crust

1. Combine the flour, sugar, salt, and lemon zest in a large bowl. In a separate small bowl, whisk the egg yolk, melted butter, and vanilla until combined.

2. Make a well in center of the flour mixture. Add the egg mixture and work together by hand until completely blended. If the mixture is not holding together, add 1 teaspoon of milk. Form the dough into a disk, wrap the dough tightly in plastic wrap, and chill in the refrigerator for at least 1 hour, or overnight.

3. To bake the crust, preheat the oven to 400 degrees F. Line the bottom of a 9-by-4-inch springform pan with a circle of parchment paper; grease the bottom and sides.

4. Remove the dough from the refrigerator. Once it has warmed just enough so that it is easily handled, transfer it to the pan. Using your fingers, press into the bottom of the pan, working the edges up onto the sides of the pan just a little; this will help avoid cream cheese leakage on the bottom of the pan. Bake for 10 minutes, or until the crust is a light golden color. Remove from the oven and let cool completely.

1 cup all-purpose flour, sifted

½ cup sugar

⅛ teaspoon salt

1 teaspoon grated lemon zest

1 egg yolk

¼ cup (½ stick) unsalted butter, melted

¼ teaspoon vanilla extract

1 teaspoon whole or 2% milk (optional)

Doughnuts

EVEN IF YOU'RE A PERSON WHO CAN'T FACE a single Monday morning without a sugar-coated doughnut paired with hot coffee, there's probably a lot you don't know about these holey rings of delicious fried dough. To start, the doughnut is very old—possibly ancient. Did you know, for instance, that petrified remains of what resemble doughnuts have been found in Native American communities in what is now the US Southwest?

. . . .

This is not to say that the art of frying dough is a uniquely American phenomenon. In fact, just about every culture has its own variation. Among the doughnut's many international relatives, you'll find *koeksisters* in South Africa, *donat kentang* in Indonesia, *sufganiyot* in Israel, *Berliner pfannkuchen* in Germany, *loukoumades* in Greece, *zeppole* in Italy, *pączki* in Poland, *malasadas* in Portugal, and *churros* in Mexico.

The American-style doughnut is most directly a descendant of the Dutch *olykoek* (that's "oily cake"). Immigrants brought the recipe to New York in the 1800s.

Washington Irving is credited with introducing the term "doughnuts" to the common vernacular in his *History of New York*, in which he describes "balls of sweetened dough, fried in hog's fat, and called doughnuts, or olykoeks." One problem with these fried rounds of dough: the center didn't seem to fry at the same rate as the outer edges. Sometimes, to offset the uneven cooking, apples, raisins or other fruit were stuffed in the center.

As much as it might hurt to admit that less is more, in the case of the doughnut, it's true: the hole in the middle promotes more even frying, ensuring that the middle is not doughy and undercooked. And when it comes to crediting the person who thought up the idea, signs point to Hanson Gregory, a seafarer

As much as it might hurt to admit that less is more, in the case of the doughnut, it's true: the hole in the middle promotes more even frying, ensuring that the middle is not doughy and undercooked.

who apparently loved telling any number of versions of the story. (See How Did Doughnuts Get Their Holes?, page 34.)

But it was going to take a lot more than a hole in the middle to make the doughnut a vital—if slightly lowbrow—part of American cuisine. And mass production was what was needed to bring the fried dough to the public eye. Up until that point, doughnuts were not primarily a breakfast food—they were a snack, sold in theaters and at carnivals. But a Russian expat living in New York City noticed the public demand for doughnuts and created the first automated doughnut machine. His machines began to sell extremely well to commercial bakeries, and at last, the supply could keep up with the demand! This spike in production coincided with coffee becoming a staple in bakeries, which certainly contributed to the doughnut's association as a morning food.

Doughnuts show no signs of slowing down in popularity—and in fact, there's been a resurgence of enthusiasm in recent years for handcrafted, small-batch doughnuts as opposed to the chain-store variety. A healthy trend, if you ask me.

Old-Fashioned Doughnuts

THESE DOUGHNUTS ARE PLEASINGLY OLD-FASHIONED TASTING and rich in flavor thanks to buttermilk and sour cream. They're a dream served warm with a dusting of confectioners' sugar, and of course, a cup of hot coffee on the side.

Makes about 18 doughnuts, plus doughnut holes

1. In a large bowl, sift together the flour, baking powder, baking soda, and salt. Set aside.

2. In another large bowl, whisk the sour cream, buttermilk, and sugar until combined. Whisk in the sugar; stir until the mixture is smooth and lump free. Beat in the eggs and vanilla just until combined, scraping down the sides of the bowl with a rubber spatula if needed.

3. In 2 to 3 increments, add the flour mixture to the buttermilk mixture, stirring with a wooden spoon just until combined. Cover and refrigerate for about 2 hours, or until completely chilled.

4. Turn the dough out on a very generously-floured surface; knead for 2 to 3 minutes, or until smooth and elastic. Let the dough chill again for about 30 minutes (this will ensure that it will not spring back when you cut it). Roll the dough out to ½-inch thickness. Cut with a floured 2-inch doughnut cutter. Set the "holes" to the side. You can also roll the doughnuts by hand for an "artisan" look.

5. In a heavy medium pot or a deep-fat fryer, put enough oil to achieve a depth of 4 inches; heat it to 375 degrees F. Fry the doughnuts, 2 or 3 at a time, until golden brown on each side (less than 3 minutes). Remove with tongs or with a slotted spoon and place on paper towels to blot excess oil. Repeat with the remaining doughnuts, making sure to let the oil return to 375 degrees F before frying a new batch.

6. Fry the doughnut holes until golden brown—they'll take less time to fry than the doughnuts.

7. Cool the doughnuts for about 5 minutes; while they're still warm, dust with confectioners' sugar. Serve warm or at room temperature; doughnuts are best eaten the day they are made.

4 cups all-purpose flour

2 teaspoons baking powder

¼ teaspoon salt

⅔ cup sour cream

⅓ cup buttermilk

¾ cup sugar

3 large eggs

1 teaspoon vanilla extract

6 to 8 cups vegetable or canola oil, for deep-fat frying

Confectioners' sugar, for dusting

HOW DID DOUGHNUTS GET THEIR HOLES?

THERE ARE MANY TALES that attempt to explain how doughnuts got their holes—one even suggests that it was the result of a Native American hunter's errant arrow, which missed its mark but speared an unlucky pilgrim's morning snack. But most tales point back to a man named Hanson Gregory.

One variation goes that, as a boy, he'd been watching his mother frying doughnuts and had noticed that the centers always remained partially uncooked and doughy. "Mother," he said, "leave a hole in the center." Laughingly, she obliged him— and never went back to the old way.

Here's another unlikely but delightful variation: Gregory enjoyed munching on a doughnut while steering his boat; one night, facing rough seas but not wanting to discard his treat, he speared it onto the spoke of his wheel, so that he'd be able to come back to it after he no longer needed both hands to steer. Another tale goes that Gregory purposely poked a hole in the doughnut to lighten it up "because he had already lost six men overboard due to the heaviness of the doughnuts."

Of course, the lore surrounding Hanson Gregory gets even more street cred based on the fact that he has a historical plaque dedicated to his invention. It's true. In Rockport, Maine, you can find a marker inscribed with the following: "In commemoration. This is the birthplace of Captain Hanson Gregory, who first invented the hole in the doughnut in 1847. Erected by his friends, Nov. 2, 1947."

Of course, it always makes me smile to hear the explanation that "the hole is so the calories can fall out." Hey, whatever it takes to help you enjoy your snack . . .

Pineapple Upside-Down Cake

THIS FESTIVE CAKE—BAKED UPSIDE-DOWN and turned before serving to reveal a circle of pineapple rings studded with maraschino cherries—is a clear example of 1950s Hawaiian kitsch, invoking idyllic fantasies of luau parties and tiki cocktails. Only one problem: The cake wasn't invented in Hawaii—it was invented in—wait for it—*Virginia*.

. . . .

Now, this is not to say that the State for Lovers invented the idea of turning a cake on its head. Upside-down baked goods preceded the famous pineapple version by many years—the art of inverting cakes to reveal toppings is a practice that dates back as far as the Middle Ages. By the 1800s in the United States, they were commonly known as skillet cakes, referring to the pan in which they were commonly baked. This method was born of necessity, in a time when ovens were not reliable for baking cakes. Putting the fruit on the bottom ensured a moist, caramelly finish; overturning the pan and letting the topping seep deliciously into the cake ensured that not a morsel would be wasted. All manner of fruits were used in these skillet cakes: pears, peaches, cherries, and famously, in the form of Tarte Tatin, apples.

There were still a few things that had to happen before upside-down desserts would become a symbol of the Donna Reed homemaker lifestyle. First, in 1901, Jim Dole established the Hawaiian Pineapple Company (now Dole Food Company, Inc.) and began marketing canned pineapple. In 1925, the company sponsored a contest calling for pineapple recipes of all kinds. They pulled out all the stops and assembled an

Putting the fruit on the bottom ensured a moist, caramelly finish; overturning the pan and letting the topping seep deliciously into the cake ensured that not a morsel would be wasted.

all-star cast of judges for the event, including staffers at the Fannie Farmer Boston Cooking School, as well as from *Good Housekeeping* and *McCall's* magazines. The prize? The recipes would be published in a cookbook titled *Hawaiian Pineapple as 100 Good Cooks Serve It*, with a $50 cash prize for each of the winners.

Here's where something amazing happened. Of the 60,000-plus submissions, a whopping 2,500 were for some variation on the pineapple upside-down cake. A few too many to call coincidence, it's clear that the concept had already been making the rounds in home kitchens. But the Dole contest gave the concept and recipe widespread visibility. The best recipe, the judges concluded, was the one submitted by one Mrs. Robert Davis of Norfolk, Virginia.

Following the contest, the recipe appeared in lots of magazine ads, and pineapple upside-down cake became a popular hostess dessert. But in the 1950s and '60s, there was a huge surge of popularity for the dessert. Why? Likely the timing: With Hawaii's statehood made official, there was sudden interest in all things Hawaiian, either real or imagined (including exaggerated tiki motifs!). And what more delicious way to celebrate the birth of a new state than with something sweet?

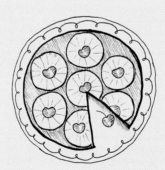

Pineapple Upside-Down Cake

EXTREMELY EASY TO PREPARE, this cake is fun to make in a clear Pyrex dish, because after baking, when you flip it over, you can witness the toppings dripping like sugary stalagmites onto the cake below. Though not necessary, it's very fun to serve the cake alongside beverages sporting mini umbrellas.

Makes one 9-inch square cake (9 servings)

1. Heat the oven to 350 degrees F. To make the topping, place the butter in a 9-inch square baking pan, and set it in the oven until melted (it's fine to do this while the oven preheats; the butter will melt quickly). Remove the pan and gently shift it so that the butter covers the entire bottom of the pan. Sprinkle the brown sugar evenly over the melted butter. Arrange the pineapple slices over the brown sugar; you should be able to comfortably fit 3 rows of 3 pineapple rings in the pan. Place a cherry in the center of each pineapple slice.

2. To make the cake, in a medium bowl, sift together the flour, baking powder, and salt. Set aside.

3. In the bowl of a stand mixer fitted with the paddle attachment, cream the butter and sugars on medium speed until fluffy, 3 to 5 minutes. Add the eggs, mixing until incorporated. Add the flour mixture alternately with the milk, in 2 to 3 additions, pausing to scrape down the sides of the bowl with a rubber spatula after each addition. Beat on low speed until fully incorporated. Pour the batter into the pan, taking care not to dislodge the pineapple or cherries.

4. Bake for 45 to 50 minutes, or until a toothpick inserted into the center of the cake comes out mostly clean. Immediately place a heatproof serving plate upside down over the pan; in one swift, sure motion, flip the plate and pan over, so that the cake is now on the serving plate. Leave the pan in place for several minutes so that the brown sugar mixture can drip over the cake. After it seems as if there is no more dripping to be done, lift off the pan. Serve while still warm. Store the cake loosely covered at room temperature for up to 2 days.

FOR THE TOPPING:

⅓ cup (5 tablespoons) butter

⅔ cup packed light brown sugar

9 slices pineapple rings in juice (from one 20-ounce can), drained

9 maraschino cherries, stems removed

FOR THE CAKE:

1½ cups all-purpose flour

1 teaspoon baking powder

½ teaspoon salt

½ cup (1 stick) butter

½ cup granulated sugar

½ cup packed light brown sugar

2 large eggs

¾ cup whole or 2% milk

Red Velvet Cake

OF ALL THE CAKES IN THE BAKERY CASE, red velvet is the flashiest: a vibrantly brazen red cake topped with a striking coat of contrasting fluffy white frosting, and a name that sounds like it could belong to an exotic dancer. In spite of its eye-catching appearance, though, the flavor is surprisingly delicate: the cake has a light cocoa and buttermilk flavor—not as assertive as many chocolate cakes, but more distinctive than a vanilla cake. It gets most of its zing from the cream cheese frosting, which is its most popular topping. It's one of those cakes that some people love and some people loathe, but everybody notices.

....

To the uninitiated, or to those who have only had an inferior version, the cake is not merely a red-tinted vanilla cake—or at least, it shouldn't be. The cake's color is a mixture of science and a sprinkling of man-made magic. A reddish hue does occur naturally, based on the chemical reaction between the alkaline ingredients (baking soda, baking powder) and the acidic ones (cocoa, buttermilk, vinegar). Of course, that natural reddish hue is a far cry from the day-glo variety we generally see today in bakeries, and that's where the magic comes in: very frequently, bakers accentuate the red with a bucket load of food coloring.

Commercially produced food coloring has been around since the early 1900s. Faced with reduced sales after the Great Depression, John Anderson Adams of Adams Extract began promoting a very red cake that elevated the red velvet cake to popular status among American housewives around the mid-century.

The "velvet" part of the cake's name was an evolution, too. As early as the Victorian era, velvet referred to the fine quality of a cake's crumb, which was enhanced by the use of cornstarch

The cake's color is a mixture of science and a sprinkling of man-made magic.

or even cocoa powder to soften the texture of the flour. Red velvet is likely a crossover: a red cake with a velvety crumb.

What tops the cake is another subject of some disagreement. Early recipes call for a boiled milk frosting, but somewhere along the line, it was eclipsed by no-cook frostings—most notably cream cheese frosting. In the 1950s, Pillsbury released a cookbook that included a recipe for a "red devil loaf," and suggested frosting it with chocolate cream cheese frosting and garnishing with pecans. By the time the cake was dubbed red velvet in the '60s, the recipes seem fairly split in terms of boiled frostings, no-cook frostings, and cream cheese frostings. So is one more authentic than the other? Not really. Recipes evolve for a reason, and the public demand for cream cheese frosting was simply higher than for other varieties—that's the way that innovations become, over time, an authentic part of recipes like this much-loved one.

Red Velvet Cake

THIS IS AN OLD-FASHIONED RED VELVET CAKE, large and lovely. I've made some updates: the recipe calls for butter instead of oil or shortening, which I believe offers a richer flavor; as for frosting the cake, I've included a recipe for both of the traditional frostings, so you can choose your own adventure. And the food coloring? Yes, it's there, and there's a lot. It's up to you how much to use—depends on whether you want a cake that whispers or one that shouts.

Makes one 8-inch layer cake (10 servings)

1. Position a rack in the center of the oven; preheat the oven to 350 degrees F. Grease and flour the bottoms and sides of 8-inch round cake pans.

2. In the bowl of a stand mixer fitted with the paddle attachment, cream the butter and sugar on medium speed until light and fluffy, 3 to 5 minutes. Add the eggs, one at a time, pausing to scrape down the sides of the bowl with a rubber spatula after each addition.

3. In a small bowl, make a paste of the food coloring and cocoa. Add this paste to the butter mixture, beating on low speed so that you don't send drops of red coloring everywhere! Add the flour alternately with the buttermilk, ensuring that each addition is fully mixed in before adding the next. Scrape down the sides of the bowl with a rubber spatula after each addition. Stir in the salt and vanilla.

4. In a separate bowl, combine the baking soda and vinegar (it will fizz up). Immediately mix it into the batter until everything is combined. Divide the batter evenly between the prepared cake pans; smooth and level the batter with an offset or rubber spatula.

5. Bake for 22 to 28 minutes, or until a cake tester inserted into the center of the cakes comes out mostly clean. Let the cakes cool in the pans for about 10 minutes; loosen the sides from the pan using a small paring knife, then turn the cakes onto a wire rack. Let cool completely before frosting.

6. To assemble, set one of the layers on a plate with its flattest side up. Spread about one-quarter of the filling on top, stopping a little short of

½ cup (1 stick) unsalted butter, softened

1½ cups sugar

2 large eggs

About 2 tablespoons red food coloring

2 heaping tablespoons unsweetened cocoa powder

2¼ cups cake flour

1 cup buttermilk

1 teaspoon salt

1 teaspoon vanilla extract

1 teaspoon baking soda

1 teaspoon white vinegar

3 cups Cream Cheese Frosting (page 16) or Boiled Milk Frosting (recipe follows)

Chocolate shavings, sprinkles, or red candies, for garnish (optional)

the outside edges of the cake. Add another layer of cake, press lightly, and repeat. Place your last cake on top and press lightly. Frost the sides and then the top of the cake with the remainder of the frosting. If desired, garnish with chocolate shavings, sprinkles, or red candies.

BOILED MILK FROSTING

 Makes about 3 cups frosting

1 cup whole milk

¼ cup all-purpose flour

1 cup (2 sticks) unsalted butter, softened

¾ cup granulated sugar

Pinch of salt

1 teaspoon vanilla extract

1. Whisk together the milk with the flour until smooth.

2. Transfer the mixture to a medium saucepan. Over medium heat, bring the mixture to a simmer, whisking continuously until it comes to a low boil. Remove the pan from the stove and transfer the hot mixture into a medium bowl; place plastic wrap directly against the milk's surface to prevent it from forming a skin. Let cool.

3. In a stand mixer fitted with the paddle attachment, cream the butter, sugar, and salt on high speed until very light and fluffy, 3 to 5 minutes. Stir in the vanilla and mix on medium speed for another 1 to 2 minutes.

4. Reduce mixer speed to low, and gradually pour the cooled milk mixture into the bowl. Increase the speed to high, and beat for 5 to 7 minutes; during this time, the frosting will become smooth and fluffy, which will give it a more pleasing texture and a more easily spreadable consistency.

ALL MIXED UP

I MAY GET IN BIG TROUBLE WITH THE SERIOUS BAKERS of the world for saying so, but I think that cake mix is a fine invention. True, the product is different than a cake made from scratch, but if the true secret ingredient is love, then cake mix has opened the door for many a timid baker to gain confidence in the kitchen. And believe it or not, playing up to the "made with love" aspect of baking is how cake mixes found an audience to begin with.

When cake mixes first debuted in the 1940s, they were a little different than they are today. They were actually far easier to assemble: all you had to do was add water, mix, and bake. And they were an utter failure. Not by the quality of the resulting baked goods necessarily, but in terms of sales.

But as I learned in *Finding Betty Crocker* by Susan Marks, General Mills made a little adjustment that added up to big results: they removed the dried egg from the mix, so that the home baker had to add a fresh egg (or eggs) before baking.

Turns out, the simple act of adding real eggs made a huge difference for home cooks: bakers felt more confident in presenting their creations as being "homemade" than their totally mixed counterparts. Of course, some naysayers will say that this was a happy accident, and that the dried egg in earlier mixes was omitted because it made the cakes stick to the pan.

Since the 1950s, cake-mix sales have exploded. They've also become popular as a "doctored" item, using recipes that start with cake mixes and then get far more elaborate from various mix-ins and clever techniques. These days, there's even more love to add to mixes: some fancier ones (that are really not much more than pre-measured, sifted dry ingredients) will ask you to add egg, butter, oil, and other ingredients. At that point, one might wonder "Why use a mix, anyway?" The simple fact is this: While some continue to loathe, many continue to love, that inimitable cake-mix flavor.

Smith Island Cake

IF YOU THINK "MARYLAND" AND "CAKE," it's likely that your first association is savory: after all, the region is legendary for their crab cakes.

. . . .

But Maryland has some great sweet cakes too—most notably the Smith Island cake, a dramatic confection composed of between eight and fifteen thin layers of yellow cake, sandwiched with a very rich chocolate icing that sets up like fudge as it cools. This toothsome fudge not only holds the layers together, but it covers the top and sides of the composed cake stack. Lovingly referred to as "frosting with the cake," the Smith Island fools the eye into thinking it's a regular layer cake—but once sliced into, the extraordinary striped interior of contrasting yellow cake and cocoa-hued filling is exposed.

The cake is named for tiny Smith Island, the only inhabited island off the coast of Maryland. Since this mini-island measures less than ten square miles, they clearly can't build out—but they can build up, and they sure do, at least in confectionery form, with this architectural marvel. It shouldn't be too surprising that this cake is the most famous culinary export from the island, and that its fame extends beyond the island to the entire region.

So who invented this amazing cake? If you ask locals, the standard response is the extremely helpful, "It's always been here." Well, "always" for Smith Island would date back to the seventeenth century, when the island was first settled by travelers from Cornwall and Wales. The settlers' ancestry is still very evident today—aside from the cake, another notable feature of the island is the local dialect, a sort of Shakespearean English similar to what's called Outer Banks brogue.

Clearly these islanders hold tight to their heritage, and this might give us a clue to the cake's origins. It's highly likely that Smith Island cake is the stateside adaptation of English tortes brought to the island by the early settlers. Perhaps

Lovingly referred to as "frosting with the cake," the Smith Island fools the eye into thinking it's a regular layer cake.

the pencil-thin layers evolved as a sweeter and lighter version of the Welsh cake, a griddlecake, because the layers do resemble pancakes more than layer cakes.

So how did it get to be so sky-high? I think it had to do with some good old-fashioned, good-natured competition. On Smith Island, a time-honored tradition is the cakewalk, a game played sort of like musical chairs, but with a cake as the prize. The participants pay to play (usually, the cakewalk is held to raise money for charity), and a prize-worthy cake is vital to the good cause. A poorly stacked cake may not attract many players and as a result, not raise as much money as a more perfectly executed one. So the bakers of Smith Island started to stack layers as a form of competition, with the most impressive cakes growing to as many as fifteen layers.

In 2008, Smith Island cake was designated the official state dessert of Maryland. It's in good company, along with the state cat (calico) and the state crustacean (blue crab)—but it probably pairs best with the state drink (milk).

In terms of timing, I suggest preparing the frosting before the cakes. This way, you can use the icing to begin assembling the layers while you bake. Doing so will keep your counter from getting too crowded, and it also keeps the cake layers nice and moist.

Smith Island Cake

TAKE A DEEP BREATH: This cake takes quite some time to make and assemble. But you'll regain all of that spent energy quickly when you see the delight on the faces of those you're serving as those magical layers are revealed . . . and even more so when you get a few bites of this over-the-top sweet treat. This recipe is adapted from the version popularized in 1981 in *Mrs. Kitching's Smith Island Cookbook*.

Makes one 9-inch 10-layer cake (16 servings)

1. Position a rack in the center of the oven; reheat the oven to 350 degrees F.

2. Gather as many 9-inch round baking pans as you can (you'll be baking 10 layers), then grease and line them with parchment paper circles. If you don't have 10 pans, you can re-use the same few pans; you'll just have to cool and clean them between batches. Have 10 sheets of parchment paper ready to let the cakes cool.

3. In a medium bowl, sift together the flour, baking powder, and salt. Set aside.

4. In a stand mixer fitted with the paddle attachment, cream the butter and sugar on medium speed until light and fluffy, about 3 to 5 minutes. Add the eggs one at a time, pausing after each addition to scrape down the sides of the bowl. Beat until smooth. Add the flour mixture, 1 cup at a time, to the butter mixture. Beat on low speed after each addition just until incorporated. With each addition, scrape down the sides of the bowl.

5. With the mixer running, pour in the evaporated milk, then the vanilla and milk. Mix just until incorporated. Pour $1/10$ of the batter into each of your prepared pans, using the back of the spoon to spread the batter evenly so that it covers the entire bottom of the pan. If you run out of batter before you've made 10 layers of cake, do not despair; you can just make thicker layers of frosting between the cake layers.

6. If you have room in your oven, bake several layers at a time for 6 to 8 minutes. You're looking for a dull finish on top and just slightly golden edges—not golden brown or crispy. Let the layers cool for a

3¼ cups cake flour

1 teaspoon baking powder

¼ teaspoon salt

1 cup (2 sticks) unsalted butter, softened

1¾ cups sugar

5 large eggs

1 cup evaporated milk

1 teaspoon vanilla extract

½ cup whole or 2% milk

6½ cups Chocolate Frosting (recipe follows)

couple of minutes in the pan before removing; then run a spatula around the edge of the pan and gently transfer the layers onto sheets of parchment paper. If it tears slightly, don't panic: you can cover up a lot with the icing.

7. To assemble, set the first slightly cooled layer on your serving plate and spread it with a thin layer of frosting, covering the entire surface of the layer. Add the next layer, frost, and repeat the process until the batter is gone (hopefully, you'll have 10 layers!). Finish by frosting the sides and then the top of the cake; I find that starting on the top, and smoothing the frosting that has dripped down the sides, is the way to go with frosting this cake.

8. Let the finished cake chill in the refrigerator for about 30 minutes before serving, so that the frosting can set. Slice while still lightly chilled. Store in the refrigerator for up to 3 days.

SMITH ISLAND FUDGE FROSTING

Makes about 6½ cups frosting

1 cup (2 sticks) unsalted butter

Two 12-ounce cans evaporated milk

⅔ unsweetened cocoa powder

8 cups confectioners' sugar

1. Melt the butter over low heat in a large saucepan. Remove from the heat, and add the cocoa powder and whisk slowly until smooth.

2. Return to the heat, this time on medium-low, and cook for approximately 10 minutes, but don't let the mixture come to a boil. Stir continuously so that it doesn't scorch. Once warm and just beginning to thicken, remove from the heat.

3. Whisk in the confectioners' sugar 1 cup at a time, until it's all incorporated. Return the pan to low heat, stirring constantly until it has thickened to the point that it forms a ribbon when you drizzle a spoonful back onto the mixture. The mixture may bubble, but don't let it boil. You want to keep the frosting slightly warm to keep it from setting in the pan; it is OK to return to low heat or add a small quantity of water to the mixture to keep it spreadable.

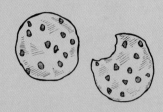

TIMELESS COOKIES & BARS

COOKIES ARE THE SYMBOL OF EVERYDAY SWEETNESS. They punctuate our daily lives: the quick snack, the cookies and milk after school, the accompaniment for afternoon tea. They can dress up for holidays too, of course—what would Christmas be without the cookies, after all? But mostly, they keep us company on a daily basis, a simple but powerful way to sprinkle a little magic on an otherwise ordinary day.

Blondies & Brownies

BLONDES MAY HAVE MORE FUN, but in the world of baked goods, blonde brownies (blondies, for short) are largely viewed as the less desirable albino cousin of the famous chocolate brownie. When you look at the history of these bar cookies, though, you'll find that we wouldn't even have brownies without their blonde sisters.

. . . .

So what's the difference? Blondies are a soft and chewy bar cookie, generally made using a vanilla or butterscotch base instead of chocolate. Although opinions will certainly differ on this subject, many agree that texture-wise, a successful blondie will fall between cakey and fudge-like: that is to say, delightfully chewy, rich, and dense. So for all of you tempted to call the blondie the bland version of the brownie: Quit it.

According to old cookbooks, blonde brownies predated chocolate brownies, though under different names. The primary ingredients of blondies (brown sugar or molasses and butter) compose butterscotch, a candy that was popular in America in the mid-nineteenth century. Cookbooks from that time contain recipes that combined traditional butterscotch ingredients with flour and a leavening agent (baking powder or baking soda); possibly these were adapted from gingerbread cake recipes. Presumably, these recipes would have produced something similar to the blonde brownies we enjoy today.

Generally, brownies fall into three categories: cakey, chewy, or fudgy; I'm pretty sure a fistfight or two has broken out over which style is superior.

Brownies, of course, are characterized by their most important ingredient: chocolate. Early recipes depended on cocoa powder; as time went on, adding melted chocolate or sometimes cocoa *and* chocolate became the favored method for attaining a deep, rich chocolate flavor. Generally, brownies fall into three categories: cakey, chewy, or fudgy; I'm pretty sure a fistfight or two has broken out over which style is superior.

Brownies are a relatively new invention. But where, you might be wondering, did they come from?

There *is* a place that claims to have dreamed up the brownie: the kitchen of Chicago's Palmer House Hotel. It happened during the 1892 Columbian Exposition, when Bertha Palmer requested that the chef make a "ladies' dessert" that would be easier to eat than a piece of pie, and make a smaller serving than a slice of layer cake. She wanted it to be included in the box lunches at the Women's Pavilion at the fair, thank you very much. What was presented was a brownie, although it's not known if that's what they were called right from the start. Apparently the reaction was good—the recipe is still served today at the Palmer House Hilton on State Street and remains a popular confection.

The 1896 edition of *The Boston Cooking-School Cook Book* was among the first known publications to feature brownies—but this version was all about little individual butterscotch-flavored cakes. However, the 1905 version of the book had a brownie redux, and this time, *they had chocolate.*

The recipe was further refined in Bangor, Maine, when a woman named Maria Willett Howard famously enriched Fannie Farmer's chocolate brownie recipe with extra egg and chocolate. This tricked-out version of the brownie was widely circulated and adopted, and is the forefather of the decadent, chewy squares that are favored today. By the 1950s, butterscotch or vanilla brownies were described as "blonde brownies," underscoring the primacy of chocolate.

Today, while blondies and brownies are both still delicious, brownies definitely dominate bakery shelves. Here is a pair of contemporary recipes for each; they're much richer than the earlier versions—but in my opinion, much more delicious.

Blondies

I THINK WE OWE IT TO THE BLONDIE to appreciate her for what she is: a deliciously toothsome, rich bar cookie with a warm and satisfying butterscotch taste. These are simple to make, with a short ingredient list that won't require a special trip to the store. I love using toasted pecans in this recipe because their buttery taste perfectly complements this bar cookie's other defining flavors.

Makes 2 dozen blondies

1. Preheat the oven to 350 F. Lightly grease a 9-by-13-inch pan. Line the bottom of the pan with parchment paper.

2. In a medium bowl, sift together the flour, baking powder, and salt.

3. In the bowl of a stand mixer fitted with the paddle attachment, beat the melted butter and brown sugar. Beat in the eggs and vanilla. Add the flour mixture in 2 or 3 additions, mixing well after each addition and pausing to scrape down the sides of the bowl with a rubber spatula between additions. Fold in the nuts.

4. Spread the batter into the prepared pan, leveling the batter using an offset or rubber spatula, level the top of the batter.

5. Bake for 25 to 30 minutes, or until a toothpick inserted into the center comes out mostly clean. If anything, it's better (taste-wise) to err on the side of slightly underbaked. Let the blondies cool completely before cutting into squares.

1¾ cups all-purpose flour

1 teaspoon baking powder

1 teaspoon salt

¾ cup (1½ sticks) unsalted butter, melted

2 cups packed dark brown sugar

3 large eggs, lightly beaten

2 teaspoons vanilla extract

1½ cups coarsely chopped toasted pecans

Brownies

THESE BROWNIES FALL FIRMLY INTO THE "FUDGE-LIKE" CATEGORY, with a crispy top. You can add chunks of chopped chocolate or lightly toasted nuts (about three-quarters cup of each would be a good place to start) if that's your style.

 Makes 2 dozen brownies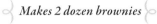

1 cup all-purpose flour

1 cup unsweetened cocoa powder

1 teaspoon salt

1½ cups (3 sticks) unsalted butter, melted

2 cups granulated sugar

¾ cup packed light brown sugar

5 large eggs, lightly beaten

2 teaspoons vanilla extract

1. Preheat the oven to 350 degrees F. Grease a 9-by-13-inch baking pan, then line it with parchment paper.

2. In a medium mixing bowl, sift together the flour, cocoa powder, and salt; set aside.

3. In the bowl of a stand mixer fitted with the paddle attachment, add the butter and the sugars; on a slow speed, beat them together until they form a cohesive, slightly gritty mixture.

4. Beat in the egg mixture in 2 to 3 additions, pausing to scrape down the sides of the bowl after each addition. Continue beating on medium speed until the mixture is smooth and fully incorporated. Beat in the vanilla. Add the flour mixture, bit by bit, beating on low speed and continuing to scrape down the sides of the bowl until well blended.

5. Spread the batter evenly into the prepared pan.

6. Bake for 40 to 45 minutes, or until a toothpick inserted into the center comes out mostly clean (it's better to underbake than to over-bake!). Let the brownies cool completely before cutting.

Chocolate Chip Cookies

CAN YOU REALLY IMAGINE A WORLD in which there is no such thing as a chocolate chip cookie? Well, believe it or not, that world existed not so very long ago: the chocolate chip cookie was only born in 1937. I know, I know. It's become such a symbol of American sweets that it's hard to imagine the pilgrims on the Mayflower not enjoying an afternoon drop cookie studded with ye olde chocolate chips, along with a glass of cold milk. How quickly it has become part of our everyday lives: a staple in bakeries across the nation, a favorite of home bakers everywhere, and really, an important symbol of American baking.

. . . .

With this cookie in particular, I find that it's helpful to view the history in a timeline format: this way, it's a little bit easier to see how the cookie has become such a big part of our lives in such a relatively short period of time. *Chocolate chip cookie, this is your life*:

1937: The chocolate chip cookie makes its first appearance. There's a famous story about the invention of the cookie by Ruth Wakefield of the Toll House Inn of Massachusetts: While preparing a batch of Butter Drop Do cookies, a favorite recipe dating back to colonial days, Wakefield cut a bar of chocolate into tiny bits and added them to her dough, expecting them to melt and make the cookies chocolate. But instead of melting, the chunks of chocolate held their shape, softening just enough to give them that particularly addictive texture and flavor that is the hallmark of the chocolate chip cookie. The resulting creation became very popular at the Inn. Soon, Wakefield's recipe was published in newspapers throughout the New England area. Regional sales of the chocolate bar skyrocketed.

1937-39: Wakefield makes a deal with the Nestlé company: she receives free chocolate for life, and they get to print her recipe on the back of their semi-sweet chocolate bar.

1939: The chocolate chip cookie is featured on the Betty Crocker radio program, *Famous Foods from Famous Places*. Suddenly, the cookie jumps from regional specialty to national superstar. It is also this year that, in an effort to make the cookies easier to make, Nestlé debuts their semisweet chocolate morsels. *Yep, you heard that right: chocolate chips were invented in response to the cookie's popularity.*

1940s: The cookie's popularity is confirmed during the war years: an article in the *Pittsburgh Post-Gazette* notes that "when the boys in service are asked about the kind of cookie they'd like to get from home, this kind still rates high . . . ."

1948: The term "smart cookie" is first documented.

1957: The phrase "That's how the cookie crumbles" is first documented.

1963: Chips Ahoy! cookies make their supermarket debut; chocolate chip cookies hit the mass market.

1969: The Cookie Monster (at this point unnamed) makes his debut on *Sesame Street*.

1977: The first Mrs. Fields cookies-only store opens in California. Shortly thereafter, a large number of franchise cookie–specific shops start opening in cities around the country.

1984: The original Toll House building burns down; the photo caption accompanying a *New York Times* article describing the fire that destroyed Ruth Wakefield's kitchen reads, "Wreckage of Toll House Restaurant in Whitman, Mass. It was where the chocolate chip cookie was invented."

1997: The chocolate chip cookie is declared the official state cookie of Massachusetts, after losing the battle for official state dessert (that honor is assigned to Boston cream pie, page 8)

Also this year, Neiman Marcus puts an end to an urban myth about their shop charging a customer $250 for their chocolate chip cookie recipe (see Urban Legend Cookie, page 171).

2013 AND BEYOND: People all over the world—especially Americans—continue their obsession with the chocolate chip cookie. It is the most popular cookie in America.

Chocolate Chip Cookies

WHAT FOLLOWS IS A RECIPE THAT'S FAIRLY LOYAL to the original Toll House–style cookie. For a real taste of the past, be sure to use chocolate cut into small chunks rather than chocolate chips—that's the way it would have been when they were invented!

 *Makes 3 dozen cookies*

1. Position 2 racks in the center of the oven; preheat the oven to 375 degrees F. Line 2 baking sheets with parchment paper and set aside.

2. In a medium bowl, stir together the flour, baking soda, and salt.

3. In a stand mixer fitted with the paddle attachment, cream the butter, sugars, and vanilla on medium speed until smooth and creamy, about 2 to 3 minutes. Add the eggs, one at a time, pausing to scrape down the sides of the bowl with a rubber spatula as needed.

4. Add the flour mixture in 2 to 3 additions and continue mixing, just until combined. Fold in the chocolate chunks and nuts by hand.

5. Using rounded tablespoons, place the dough onto your prepared baking sheets, leaving 1½ inches on all sides to allow for spreading. Bake for 8 to 10 minutes, or until golden brown at the edges and set in the middle. Cool on the baking sheets for 5 minutes before transferring the cookies to wire racks to cool completely.

6. Store the cookies at room temperature in an airtight container for up to 7 days.

2⅓ cups all-purpose flour

1 teaspoon baking soda

1 teaspoon salt

1 cup (2 sticks) unsalted butter, softened

½ cup granulated sugar

1 cup packed light brown sugar

2 teaspoons vanilla extract

2 large eggs

16 ounces semisweet chocolate, cut into small chunks (about 2 cups)

1 cup chopped, toasted walnuts or pecans

Peanut Butter Cookies

YOU KNOW THESE COOKIES WELL: those fat peanut buttery rounds, flattened and tattooed with the signature crosshatch marks from the tines of a fork. But while they're about as classic and recognizable as a cookie can possibly get, the all-American peanut butter cookie is actually a relatively recent baked innovation.

. . . .

This cookie wouldn't be much more than a plain old sugar cookie if it weren't for its key ingredient: peanut butter. Grinding peanuts to form a foodstuff had been practiced in health sanitariums in the late 1800s, and was part of the new foods unveiled at the St. Louis World's Fair of 1904. It had even been promoted as a healthful substitute for butter or shortening in various recipes.

But the man who is credited with really bringing peanut butter to the public eye is George Washington Carver. This Renaissance man was not only an instructor at the first African American college, the Tuskegee Institute, he was also a botanist and scientist; perhaps his most lasting legacy, though, is as a peanut pioneer. It was he who promoted the peanut as a viable crop in the American South, not only educating people on how to cultivate it, but also by offering hundreds of uses for the legume. While peanut butter had not been invented at the time of his 1916 volume, *How to Grow the Peanut and 105 Ways of Preparing it for Human Consumption*, Carver clearly understood that peanuts and desserts made a pleasurable combination, based on the fact that among the volume's recipes (more than half of which are sweets) are those for peanut layer cake, peanut doughnuts, peanut pudding, peanut nougat, peanut taffy, and peanut roll cake with jelly.

By the early 1930s, peanut butter cookies were streaming forth from the ovens of America's home bakers, and in 1932 the iconic waffle-like fork marks were officially added.

The process of grinding peanuts was refined by a gentleman named Joseph Rosefield, who churned the peanuts like butter, which resulted in a very creamy product. He held the first patent for shelf-stable peanut butter.

By the early 1930s, peanut butter cookies were streaming forth from the ovens of America's home bakers, and in 1932 the iconic waffle-like fork marks were officially added. The practice of using the tines of a fork to flatten a cookie had been practiced for decades, but it was the *Schenectady Gazette* that published a recipe adding the fork marks specifically to peanut butter cookies. Not long after, Pillsbury made the practice commonplace by including the fork-press in the directions. Today, it's hardly a peanut butter cookie if you don't do this, and plus, how else can you tell them apart from all the others in the cookie jar?

Interestingly, Pillsbury is also connected to the success of the Peanut Butter Blossom, a famous variation of the peanut butter cookie where, instead of being pressed with a fork, the cookie is flattened by pressing a Hershey's Kiss in the center. This cookie was entered in the Pillsbury Bake-Off of 1957. It didn't win a prize, but it certainly captured the public's attention; now it's a cookie that you'll see at almost every cookie swap and bake sale.

Oh, and don't forget to file away in your memory that June 12 is National Peanut Butter Cookie Day.

Peanut Butter Cookies

THESE COOKIES TASTE EVEN BETTER the day after baking, as the peanut buttery flavor really takes over. To enhance these old-fashioned favorites in a very stylish, up-to-date way, try sprinkling just a few grains of coarse sea salt on each cookie before baking. That little hit of crunchy salt takes those familiar flavors that we love to another level entirely.

 Makes about 2 dozen cookies

2½ cups all-purpose flour

½ teaspoon baking soda

⅛ teaspoon salt

1 cup (2 sticks) unsalted butter, softened

1¼ cups creamy peanut butter (hydrogenated or "no-stir")

1 cup granulated sugar

1 cup packed light brown sugar

2 large eggs

1. Preheat the oven to 375 degrees F. Line 2 baking sheets with parchment paper and set aside.

2. Sift together the flour, baking soda, and salt. Set to the side.

3. In a stand mixer fitted with the paddle attachment, mix the butter and peanut butter at medium-high speed until light and fluffy, 3 to 5 minutes. Add the sugars; beat well, until smooth and creamy. Add in the eggs, one by one, mixing well after each addition.

4. Mix in the dry ingredients in 2 to 3 additions, scraping down the sides of the bowl with a rubber spatula as needed to ensure the batter is well combined. Roll the dough into small (1-inch) balls; place on the prepared baking sheet. Flatten with a fork dipped in sugar (to keep it from sticking), aligning the tines first in one direction and then the other to form a crosshatch pattern.

5. Bake for 10 to 12 minutes, or until golden brown on the edges. Let the cookies cool on the pans for several minutes before transferring to a wire rack to cool completely. Store in an airtight container for up to 7 days.

Puffed Rice Treats

JUST ABOUT EVERY AMERICAN CITIZEN has enjoyed a bar cookie of some sort made with cereal, and it all started with the Rice Krispie Treat. Technically, the Rice Krispie Treat is not a baked good: it's made on top of your stove or in the microwave. But honorary baked good–status is warranted for these no-bake squares of cereal puffs bound together with a gooey marshmallow and butter mixture, since they so comfortably share real estate with other American icons such as brownies and chocolate chip cookies at most bakeries and bake sales, and because there's a truly sweet story behind how they became such a beloved member of the baked good in-crowd.

. . . .

These treats certainly wouldn't have been so popular without Rice Krispies, the cereal that is their main ingredient. The cereal debuted in 1928 and was marketed as a health cereal. "Snap, crackle, and pop" treats took a while to catch on, but the idea of cereal squares wasn't new: both in 1916 and 1938, dessert books featuring cereal treats were published—the latter book included a recipe for something called Puffed Wheat Squares, which included dry cereal, butter, sugar, molasses, and vinegar.

But then it all came together, thanks to two ladies from Michigan named Mildred Day and Malitta Jensen. Although you might not be familiar with their names, if you've ever enjoyed a Rice Krispie Treat, you should pause and take a moment to say "thank you." Day was a Kellogg's employee. Faced with organizing a fundraiser for a Campfire Girls troop, she and Jensen cleverly adapted the older cereal-based recipes for her target audience. Why use marshmallows? Proximity was key: during that era, a popular fundraiser was selling Campfire Marshmallows in a box, similar to

Marshmallow treats were popular with both children, who loved to eat them, and with mothers, who liked how cheap and easy they were to make.

the Girl Scout cookie drives of today. Day wisely decided to remove the molasses and vinegar from the recipe and add marshmallows to the mix; instead of a generic puffed-grain cereal, she used Rice Krispies.

All of this happened during the summer of 1939, in a small town in Michigan. And Michigan was a very receptive audience: The Kellogg's company was much loved in the area; they'd proven to be strong supporters of their employees and the community during the Great Depression and World War II. So Day's clever product adaptation appealed to the community on several important levels, and the treats quickly went from regional specialty to national superstar.

Marshmallow treats were popular both with children, who loved to eat them, and with mothers, who liked how cheap and easy they were to make. It didn't take long for Kellogg's to take notice and add the recipe to the back of the Rice Krispies cereal box. And so the legacy of Mildred Day lives on. When she died in 1996, she was given full credit as the inventor of the treats.

Puffed Rice Treats

I DARE YOU TO MESS UP THIS INCREDIBLY EASY, NO-BAKE RECIPE. The resulting treats will undoubtedly bring on a wave of fond memories. Feel free to make them fancier: use different cereals, brown your butter and add a sprinkling of sea salt, or add a few drops of food coloring for special holidays. But here's your foundation.

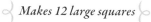

Makes 12 large squares

1. Generously grease a 9-by-13-inch baking pan. Set aside.

2. In a very large saucepan, melt the butter and salt over low heat. Once melted, add the marshmallows. Stir the marshmallows as they melt to prevent them from scorching and turning brown. Remove the pan from the heat. Add the cereal; using a wooden spoon, stir until evenly coated.

3. Turn the mixture out into the baking pan. Using a buttered spatula (or your hand, with a sheet of wax paper), press the mixture into the pan, patting it down to ensure that it is nicely packed and fairly even and flat on top. Let cool completely and cut into squares.

4. Store in an airtight container in a single layer or with layers divided by wax or parchment paper for up to 5 days.

½ cup (1 stick) unsalted butter

¼ teaspoon salt

1 bag (about 10.5 ounces) miniature marshmallows

7 cups puffed rice cereal

Whoopie Pies

PIE? MY EYE. THIS IS ACTUALLY A COOKIE: a particularly cakey sort, sandwiched with a rich, sweet filling. It's sometimes called a Gob—and there's even a small contingent that refers to the treat as the BFO (Big Fat Oreo). Sadly, my own name for them, Sweetburgers (referring to the fact that, at least in shape, the sandwich cookies resemble a hamburger on a bun), has yet to take off.

. . . .

While the classic version will always feature chocolate cookies, there's some argument as to what should go in the middle. Marshmallow fluff is favored in New England, whereas a sweet "creme," often made with shortening, is more popular elsewhere. But the whoopie pie is constantly evolving, and now bakeries are commonly offering all sorts of varieties, from pumpkin to red velvet to banana or gingerbread.

But even more interesting than its construction is the fact that this seemingly innocent cookie-cake has caused a sort of sugary civil war between Maine and Pennsylvania, who both argue that the other state stole the treat in a case of "confectionery larceny."

Pennsylvanians claim that the treat is an Amish invention. It evolved, they say, as a way to use cake batter leftovers; when these cake-wiches were discovered in a lunch pail, they'd cause the jubilant cry of "Whoopie!" The "pie" part would have been derived from hand pie, referring to the treats as being handheld. A tradition that's orally handed down through the generations, this story is hard to document with a paper trail.

Maine can actually cite specific dates. Labadie's Bakery, located in the same spot since 1925, claims to be the oldest spot in the United States selling whoopie pies continuously. Mainers also put their love on paper: in 2011, the whoopie pie was sworn in as the official state treat. Don't confuse it with the official state dessert, however—that honor goes to Maine blueberry pie.

Whoopie Pies

REGARDLESS OF ITS HAZY ORIGINS, the final verdict is that this scrumptious sandwich cookie is loved by all. Here's a recipe for the classic version of this treat: pillowy chocolate cookies encasing a sweet dream of creamy marshmallow filling.

Makes twelve 2½-inch sandwiches

CHOCOLATE COOKIES:

2 cups all-purpose flour, plus 1 tablespoon

½ cup unsweetened cocoa powder

1 teaspoon baking soda

1 teaspoon salt

1 cup sugar

¾ cup unsalted butter, softened

2 large eggs

2 teaspoons vanilla extract

¾ cup whole or 2% milk

CREAM FILLING:

¾ cup unsalted butter, softened

1½ cups marshmallow fluff

1 teaspoon vanilla extract

1½ cups confectioners' sugar

1. Preheat the oven to 350 degrees F. Line 2 baking sheets with parchment paper and set aside.

2. To make the cookies, sift together the flour, cocoa powder, baking soda, and salt in a medium-size bowl. Set aside.

3. In a stand mixer fitted with the paddle attachment, cream the butter and sugar on medium speed for 3 minutes. Mix in the egg and vanilla. Add the dry ingredients bit by bit, alternating with the milk, and scraping the bowl with a rubber spatula as needed, until the batter is smooth.

4. Using either a 1-tablespoon cookie scoop or by heaping tablespoons, drop 12 rounds of cookie dough on each baking sheet, leaving about 1½ inches of space around each mound of dough.

5. Bake until the cookies have a dull finish and spring back when touched lightly, 8 to 10 minutes.

6. Let the cookies cool on the sheets for about 5 minutes, then use a metal spatula to transfer them to a wire rack to cool completely.

7. To make the cream filling, combine the butter, marshmallow fluff, and vanilla in a medium bowl; beat with an electric mixer on high speed until smooth, 3 to 5 minutes. Reduce speed to low, and add the sugar gradually. Increase the speed to high, and beat until very fluffy, 2 to 3 minutes.

8. Spread a generous amount of filling on a cooled cookie and top with another cookie.

9. Wrap individually in plastic wrap, or store in a single layer in an airtight container for up to 3 days.

TRADITIONAL PIES

I FIRMLY BELIEVE THAT STRESS CANNOT EXIST in the presence of a pie. It's a humble representation of hearth and home, a cozy, comforting food that cannot be rushed in preparation; once ready, it beckons you to sit down and stay a while. And it's often paired with ice cream, which is never a bad thing! These pies range from simple to extravagantly rich, but a bite of any of them is an invitation to slow down and taste a simpler time, if just for a moment.

Apple Pie

APPLE PIE IS CONSIDERED *THE* **QUINTESSENTIAL** American dessert. But truthfully, it's about as American as Winston Churchill.

. . . .

Pies have been around for a very, *very* long time. American pies are a fairly direct descendant of the ones made in medieval Europe, sweetly referred to as "coffins" because the crust was considered a final resting place for the delicious contents. While most pies of that era were savory, apples were one of the few exceptions: recipes for apples baked in a pastry crust date as far back as the 1300s. The earliest apple pies didn't have added sugar, but they did contain spices. While perhaps not served as a dessert per se, they would have been naturally sweeter than a savory meat pie.

When the Dutch got their hands on apples and pastry, they made wonderful things happen. A recipe surprising similar to our modern apple pie was commonplace in the culture by the 1600s—you can see it for yourself in still-life paintings of the era.

This is all to say that clearly, apples have been widely embraced as a pie filling since well before Europeans began settling in the New World. Those early settlers tried their hand at apple pie using crabapples, the only apple native to North America (results, I hear, were iffy). Additional varieties of apples were planted by the colonists fairly early on, though, and by the time they were in regular crop rotation, the idea of sweet pies had already developed widely in the area. By the 1700s, apple pie was a common food on the East Coast; what's interesting, though, is that it wasn't traditionally eaten for dessert. Early on, it was a popular dinner for children, and a common breakfast or breakfast accompaniment for farmers.

So referring to something as being "as American as apple pie" isn't quite a lie. Because like the settlers, apple pie was a foreigner reborn in the new land, or, as it is aptly put by the American Pie Council, pie was "transformed into a distinctly American experience."

Another aspect that has contributed to the popularity of this pie is the fact that fresh apples are nearly always available in markets,

American pies are a fairly direct descendant of the ones made in medieval Europe, sweetly referred to as "coffins" because the crust was considered a final resting place for the delicious contents.

and when they're not, dried apples will work, too. Even without apples, you can make something called mock apple pie. Perhaps you remember this one from chemistry class (that's where I first made it) or have come upon it as a curiosity: it's a pie made with crackers, usually Ritz, combined with syrup and spices to taste like apple pie. It's oddly effective. While one might believe that it's an invention of cracker companies, the recipe dates back to the nineteenth century, when American pioneers, short on fresh apples, came up with this innovative way to make the pie without fruit. Their secret? Soda crackers. In 1935, just one year after Ritz Crackers were introduced to the public, the recipe enjoyed a resurgence and became associated with the brand. This recipe has become a classic in its own right—though perhaps more as a novelty than as a serious rival for fresh apple pie.

One last idea for you, if you prefer your pie spicy-sweet: a popular way to give it a little kick is by adding about one-third cup of cinnamon candies in place of the ground cinnamon. Not only is the flavor compelling, but they impart the prettiest pink color to the pie.

Apple Pie

THIS DOUBLE-CRUSTED WONDER is filled with tart apples baked in their own juices, with a kiss of sugar. Serve with a wedge of sharp Vermont cheddar, a scoop of creamy vanilla ice cream, or just straight up, with a milk "back."

Makes one 9-inch double-crust pie (8 servings)

Dough for one 9-inch double-crust piecrust, rolled and cut, homemade or store-bought

6 to 7 medium Granny Smith apples, peeled, cored, and sliced into 16 pieces each

¾ cup sugar, plus more for sprinkling

1 teaspoon grated lemon zest

Juice of 1 lemon (about 2 tablespoons)

2 teaspoons ground cinnamon

½ teaspoon ground nutmeg

⅛ teaspoon ground cloves

2 tablespoons all-purpose flour

2 tablespoons unsalted butter, cut into ¼-inch pieces

1 large egg beaten with 1 tablespoon water, for egg wash

1. Preheat the oven to 350 degrees F. Line a 9-inch pie pan with one of the pastry circles, pressing it into the bottom and sides of the pan.

2. In a large bowl, combine the apple slices, sugar, lemon zest, lemon juice, spices, and flour. Toss well.

3. Spoon the apples into the pie pan, along with any juices that may have collected. Dot the fruit with the butter, and cover with the remaining pastry circle. Cut several steam vents across top. Seal the edges by crimping them in your signature pattern. Brush the top crust with the egg wash and sprinkle with additional sugar.

4. Bake for 45 to 55 minutes, or until the top crust is golden and the juices are bubbling.

5. Transfer the pie to a wire rack to cool completely before serving. Serve at room temperature or slightly warmed, preferably with ice cream or whipped cream (or both; heck, apples are health food!) on the side.

Nutty Chocolate Pie

I'M FAIRLY CERTAIN THAT NO ONE would disagree that a shortcrust pastry filled with a rich chocolate-nut-caramel filling is an extremely delicious and enjoyable treat. In fact, if anything, it's almost too good, practically begging you to eat another slice . . . or ten.

. . . .

However, you will face a big-time objection of the legal variety if you try to bake this pie and call it Derby-Pie®, which is one of the most famous versions of this dessert. Because unless you're a member of the Kern family that invented the pie and holds the trademark, you do not know the secret recipe—and you might just have a lawsuit on your hands.

It all began in the 1950s when Walter and Leaudra Kern, owners of the Melrose Inn of Prospect, Kentucky, created a specialty dessert. Assisted by their son George, they tested and tweaked and retested their recipe, finally settling on the ultimate version of their nutty-chocolaty-gooey creation. The name was chosen by virtue of sweet serendipity: after reaching an impasse (with every family member having a different idea for the name), they all put their names in a hat; the chosen slip of paper read "Derby Pie."

In 1969 the Kerns trademarked their recipe, along with its name. (The hyphen and trademark symbol are part of the name—so get it right: it's Derby-Pie®.) The trademark wasn't strongly enforced until the late 1970s, when the Kern's grandson, Alan Rupp, took over the business and began religiously defending the trademark. Now, by that time, wannabe recipes had found their way into various cookbooks far and wide. Part of Rupp's job included challenging publications that featured a similar pie and used the family's trademarked name. In 1982, the company

Even local restaurants and bakeries now call their pies by other, non-infringing names, including but not limited to Triple Crown Pie, Winner's Pie, Race Day Pie, and (my favorite) Pegasus Pie.

even went after a self-published local cookbook (you know the kind: with the plastic spiral binding and recipes from all your favorite neighbors), demanding that the book be recalled so that the page with the recipe could be removed.

Bon Appétit had a victory later in the '80s when a judge deemed Derby-Pie® generic, but the decision was later reversed. Even packaged-food giant Nestlé was sued at one point. Laugh if you'd like, but the Kerns have a reputation for winning these lawsuits. As a result, even local restaurants and bakeries now call their pies by other, non-infringing names, including but not limited to Triple Crown Pie, Winner's Pie, Race Day Pie, and (my favorite) Pegasus Pie.

Why be so protective of the name? While one might argue that they should just let it slide, it can't be denied that trademarks lose strength if what they stand for is allowed to erode and change on the whims of others. The Derby-Pie® recipe is still fiercely protected by the Kerns—it's baked only on their premises, and sold to approved retailers and via mail order. And more power to them: while the basic elements of the pie are easily recognizable, no one has ever been able to exactly duplicate their special filling and delicate crust.

This recipe is not for the genuine Derby-Pie®. I'm certainly not privy to the top-secret recipe, and truly, if you want that unique taste experience, you're going to have to buy one for yourself—or better yet, visit them in Kentucky. But what I can share is a recipe for a pie that is a downright naughty indulgence and will certainly whet your appetite for sweetness.

Nutty Chocolate Pie

THIS IS BASICALLY A PECAN PIE (a really good pecan pie) with all its glorious amenities: booze, toasted nuts, and that awesome slightly jelly-like brown sugary filling. But it really goes over the top with the addition of chocolate chips (or your favorite semi- or bittersweet chocolate bar, chopped into small pieces) sprinkled in the bottom of the pan. The chocolate softens but doesn't quite melt into the delicious filling.

Makes one 9-inch pie (8 to 10 servings)

1. Preheat the oven to 325 degrees F.

2. Roll the pie dough into a circle about 12 inches in diameter; place it into a 9-inch pie pan and crimp the edges (or use a commercial frozen pie shell). Sprinkle the nuts and chocolate evenly onto the bottom of the piecrust; set aside.

3. In a large saucepan, combine the corn syrup, sugars, and bourbon, and bring to a boil over medium heat. Once boiling, cook for 2 to 3 minutes, stirring constantly to avoid scorching. Remove from the heat.

4. In a medium bowl, whisk together the eggs, butter, cornstarch, vanilla, and salt. Slowly pour about one-quarter of the hot mixture into the egg mixture, whisking constantly (if you add the hot syrup too quickly, the eggs will cook). Add the remaining hot mixture, continuing to whisk. If you notice any small lumps in the mixture, strain through a mesh sieve. Pour the filling slowly over the nuts and chocolate, being careful not to move them around within the piecrust.

5. Bake for 50 to 55 minutes, or until set in the center; cool on a wire rack. Serve the pie at room temperature with whipped cream or ice cream, if desired. To store the pie, wrap it tightly and refrigerate for up to 5 days.

Dough for one 9-inch piecrust, homemade or store-bought

¾ cup chopped toasted walnut

¾ cup chopped toasted pecans

8 ounces (about 1 cup) semi-sweet chocolate morsels

1 cup dark corn syrup

½ cup granulated sugar

½ cup firmly packed light brown sugar

¼ cup rum, bourbon, or water

3 large eggs

¼ cup (½ stick) butter, melted

2 teaspoons cornstarch

2 teaspoons vanilla extract

½ teaspoon salt

Lemon Meringue Pie

LEMON MERINGUE PIE IS POSSIBLY THE MOST DRAMATIC dessert in the diner dessert case: a rich, neon-yellow custard pie topped with a sky-high cloud of lightly-crisp-on-the-edges meringue. Who could even dream up such a pie, visually more like an avant-garde art object than a digestible dessert? As it turns out, it's really three separate dishes that were ingeniously combined as one.

. . . .

First on the scene was meringue, which had been kicking around since the 1600s. Then came the filling. Lemon desserts had been prepared in America since even before nation's formation: Columbus brought lemon seeds with him on his journeys, and the Spanish planted lemons in what is now California. As for the custard, per the *Food Journal of Lewis & Clark*, the Quakers received credit for developing lemon custard recipes in the late 1700s, and the concept became popular and more widespread in the early 1800s. Given their fondness for pies, it wouldn't be too crazy to imagine that the Quakers could see the beauty in plopping down some of that beautiful, tangy custard into one of their delicious piecrusts.

Today, it's a dessert that embraces a bit of high culture in low-priced eateries, and remains a unique sweet-tart favorite in this great land of ours.

But it was a city girl named Elizabeth Coane Goodfellow who deserves credit for taking this dessert to sky-high levels of delight when she brought the custard and the meringue together in delicious pie matrimony. Goodfellow was an interesting lady: American pastry cook, confectioner, and cooking school instructor—and, legend has it, ancestor of Jacqueline Kennedy Onassis. She was married three times, and her third marriage, to a clockmaker in Philadelphia, brought her to the city, where she started a cooking school—not a common thing for a lady to do in the early 1800s. Nobody knows where she honed her skills as a cook, but apparently she was quite good: among other accomplishments, she was a mentor to Eliza Leslie, whose books went on to become extremely influential early-American cookbooks. Although Goodfellow never published her own book, she is remembered for something far more delicious: introducing lemon meringue pie.

The concept was featured in Eliza Leslie's popular books, and it didn't take long for this early version of the pie to spread far and wide. It caught like fire across the northeast, notably at the Parker House Hotel (also the home of the Boston cream pie, page 8), where it was perfected. From there, it gained popularity in commercial kitchens before finding its place in American diners. Today, it's a dessert that embraces a bit of high culture in low-priced eateries, and remains a unique sweet-tart favorite in this great land of ours.

Lemon Meringue Pie

THIS RECIPE CALLS FOR A CRUST that uses vegetable shortening: while one might make a good argument for the superior taste of an all-butter crust, I urge you to try this one, using at least part shortening, to get the real diner-style piecrust experience. I find that while you get a slightly less flaky crust with the shortening, it is very tender—and it acts a bit like a sponge, absorbing the flavors of the lemon custard in a very nice way. Though optional, a few drops of yellow food coloring add a little "oomph" to the naturally pale yellow cake.

 *Makes one 9-inch pie (8 servings)*

1. Preheat the oven to 400 degrees F.

2. In a small bowl, beat the egg yolks with a fork. Set aside.

3. Whisk together the sugar and cornstarch in a medium saucepan. Add the water. Cook over medium heat, stirring frequently. Let it come to a boil; stir constantly for 1 minute at the boiling point. It will begin to thicken. Remove from the heat.

4. Immediately pour about one-quarter of the hot mixture into the egg yolks; when well combined, pour this mixture back into the saucepan. Boil and stir for 2 minutes; remove from the heat. Add the butter, lemon zest, lemon juice, and food coloring. Stir until the butter is melted and everything is well combined. Pour the hot filling into the piecrust.

5. Prepare the meringue topping, then spoon it onto the filling. Spread it evenly over the filling, carefully sealing the meringue to the edges of the crust to prevent shrinking or weeping. Using a knife, form the top of the meringue into little peaks (think punk hairdo) or make swirls on the top for a pretty finish.

6. Bake for 8 to 12 minutes, or until the meringue is light brown. Set the pie on a wire cooling rack and allow to cool in a draft-free place for about 2 hours. Cover and refrigerate the cooled pie until serving. Store any leftover pie in the refrigerator for up to 2 days.

4 egg yolks

1½ cups sugar

⅓ cup cornstarch

1½ cups water

3 tablespoons unsalted butter, softened and cut into pieces

2 teaspoons finely grated lemon zest

½ cup freshly squeezed lemon juice

2 to 3 drops yellow food coloring (optional)

One 9-inch Piecrust (recipe follows)

3½ cups Meringue Topping (recipe follows)

1 cup all-purpose flour

½ teaspoon salt

⅓ cup plus 1 tablespoon shortening (can use part butter), chilled

2 to 3 tablespoons ice-cold water

PIECRUST

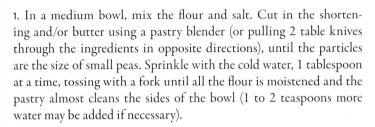

Makes one 9-inch crust

1. In a medium bowl, mix the flour and salt. Cut in the shortening and/or butter using a pastry blender (or pulling 2 table knives through the ingredients in opposite directions), until the particles are the size of small peas. Sprinkle with the cold water, 1 tablespoon at a time, tossing with a fork until all the flour is moistened and the pastry almost cleans the sides of the bowl (1 to 2 teaspoons more water may be added if necessary).

2. Gather the pastry into a ball. On a lightly floured surface, shape it into a flattened round. Wrap in plastic wrap; refrigerate for about 45 minutes, or until the dough is firm and cold, yet pliable. (Chilling the dough allows the shortening to become slightly firm, which helps make the baked pastry flakier.) If refrigerated longer, let the pastry soften slightly before rolling.

3. Using a floured rolling pin, roll the dough into a circle about 12 inches in diameter, dusting the board and the top of the dough as needed to prevent sticking. Fold the pastry into fourths; center it in a 9-inch pie pan. Unfold the dough and ease it into plate, pressing firmly against the bottom and sides. Trim any overhanging dough so that it extends about 1 inch from the rim of the pie pan. Fold the edge of the dough under, making it even with plate. Press together, then flute or crimp the edge decoratively as desired. Prick the bottom and sides of the dough thoroughly with a fork. Freeze the pastry until it is hard—about 30 minutes.

4. Preheat the oven to 475 degrees F.

5. Bake for 8 to 10 minutes, or until light brown; cool on a wire rack.

4 egg whites

¼ teaspoon cream of tartar

⅓ cup sugar

½ teaspoon vanilla extract

MERINGUE TOPPING

Makes 3½ cups meringue

1. In a very clean medium bowl, beat the egg whites and cream of tartar with an electric mixer on high speed until foamy. Add the sugar 1 tablespoon at a time, followed by the vanilla, and continue beating until stiff and glossy.

Pecan Pie

HERE'S A FUN LITTLE FACT: "pecan" is a Native American word used to describe "nuts requiring a stone to crack." It's true. But as hard as those nuts might be to crack, it's worth the effort, because they are the very heart of that sticky, make-your-teeth-hum-and-your-soul-buzz-with-sweetness dessert known as pecan pie.

. . . .

The long road from discovery to pie production began with a little nut that could: the pecan. It's actually the only major tree nut that is native to North America. Pecans were used by Native Americans, then cultivated by Spanish settlers in Mexico. When French and Spanish colonists along the Gulf of Mexico began raising and exporting the pecan, it became a worldwide phenomenon. Its popularity spread as it became more widely available, and the nut quickly became a staple in the gardens of such folks as George Washington and Thomas Jefferson.

It is the aforementioned French settlers who brought the pecan to New Orleans, which was to become Pecan Central: the climate was favorable for growing the nuts, water was plentiful, and distribution venues made it a great choice. For a time, revenues from the pecan harvest were more valuable than cotton.

But let's get back to arguably the finest use of pecans: as a decadent filling for pies. During the pecan's early days in the southern United States, a few things happened. First, the French connection: Pralines, an almond and caramelized sugar confection, were reimagined stateside with pecans and became very popular in the New Orleans area. Considering this, the jump from confection to pie wasn't so drastic, and the pie proved popular in the region: an early recipe called Texas Pecan Pie appeared in

When French and Spanish colonists along the Gulf of Mexico began raising and exporting the pecan, it became a worldwide phenomenon.

Ladies' Home Journal in 1897. The recipe, which called for a custard base as well as pecans soaked in milk, is clearly an ancestor—but it's not quite the pie we think of today.

And then, along came Karo, the corn syrup company. According to company lore, a sales executive's wife discovered a new use for corn syrup when she combined it with sugar, eggs, vanilla, and pecans, and baked it in a pie shell. Sheer brilliance! (In the South, the recipe was and still is called Karo Pie.) And so a debt of gratitude must be paid, yes, to corn syrup. Pecan pie soon made its debut in such well-known cookbooks as *The Boston Cooking-School Cook Book* and *The Joy of Cooking*.

Pecan Pie

UNBELIEVABLY RICH, this pie has gained special-occasion status, and tends to be most popular around the holidays as a dense, comforting cold-weather dessert. When making this pie, the only fussy part of the recipe is tempering the eggs; if you do it too quickly, you could end up a scramble in your sweet mixture. But don't stress. Take a deep breath, beat like heck, and keep your eyes on the prize: a delicious pie at the end of that baking road.

Makes one 9-inch pie (8 to 10 servings)

1. Preheat the oven to 325 degrees F.

2. Roll the pie dough into a circle about 12 inches in diameter; place it into the pie pan and crimp the edges (or use a commercial frozen pie shell). Keep the dough refrigerated while you prepare the filling.

3. Put the corn syrup and brown sugar in a heavy saucepan over medium heat and cook, stirring occasionally, until the sugar dissolves. The mixture will bubble lightly.

4. Remove from the heat and add the butter, water, and vanilla. Let the mixture cool to warm, then slowly add the eggs and whisk vigorously until smooth (don't add the eggs while the mixture is still very hot, or you'll have scrambled eggs!).

5. Arrange the pecans on the bottom of the crust. Carefully pour the filling over them (some will magically rise to the top). Bake for 45 to 50 minutes, or until the filling is set. What to do if the crust is browning more rapidly than the insides are setting up? Cover the edges with foil, and the crust will not brown so quickly. Let the pie cool completely before slicing.

6. To store the pie, wrap it tightly and refrigerate for up to 5 days.

Dough for one 9-inch piecrust, homemade or store-bought

1 cup light corn syrup

¾ cup packed dark brown sugar

2 tablespoons unsalted butter

2 tablespoons water

1 teaspoon vanilla extract

3 large eggs

2 cups coarsely chopped pecans, lightly toasted

Pumpkin Pie

THIS EARTHY, COMFORTING, SPICE-INFUSED PIE is the perfect intersection of mellow pumpkin and rich custard, served in a flaky crust; a cozier late-autumn treat would be hard to imagine. Today, its presence at the Thanksgiving table is practically a requirement.

. . . .

When it comes to the history of the pumpkin pie, there's a little fate and a little free will involved. Like all American pies, this one is a descendant of medieval crusts designed merely as vessels for fillings. At that time, the crust wasn't the best part of the package: after being baked without a pan, in the embers of a fire, it tended to become . . . well, pretty crusty and inedible. But, it did protect the contents, usually savory, on hunting trips and voyages from here to there. Over the years, pie-making methods improved, and the size of a typical pie increased—they had to be pretty big, after all, to fit four and twenty blackbirds!

Meanwhile, in what would one day be called the United States, pumpkins were a staple food for many Native Americans. The shells were cut into strips, dried, and made into mats, or left whole to be used as bowls; the innards were roasted by the fire and eaten. A useful little gourd indeed.

As the first settlers came to America from Europe, they learned to love some types of local produce out of necessity: it was that, or not eat. Pumpkin was one such food, which quickly entered their cooking repertoire.

In 1796, *American Cookery* by Amelia Simmons was published. This was the first truly American cookbook—that is to say, written and published in America, and using ingredients native to America—and through this text, it's clear that pumpkin was by then a staple food. The volume

The first Thanksgiving feasts were celebrations of having "made it" in the New World, and the pumpkin pie is a wholesome symbol of freedom and survival.

contains several recipes for "pumpkin" puddings, which were made by combining stewed pumpkin, cream, eggs, sugar, and what at the time were very exotic spices (cinnamon, nutmeg, etc.). Really, not such a far stretch from today's pumpkin pie filling. After that, it didn't take too long for old-world customs to meet up with this new-school vegetable, and the sweet pumpkin mixture was soon being poured into pastry crusts.

The first Thanksgiving feasts were celebrations of having "made it" in the New World, and the pumpkin pie is a wholesome symbol of freedom and survival.

In the 1900s, two separate factors contributed to the continued evolution of the pie: the growing use of evaporated milk, and the rising popularity of back-of-the-box recipes. These two developments came together thanks to Charles Scott Bridges, who may have been the best thing to ever happen to canned pumpkin. He spent the better part of his life in the employment of Libby's canned food company, eventually becoming the company's president and chief executive officer. He expanded the company largely through innovation: engaging the customer through promotion of the company's products as ingredients proved particularly successful, and Libby's back-of-the-label pumpkin pie became one of the nation's most popular. Apparently it paid off for Libby's: sales of canned pumpkin skyrocketed, and the recipe is still one of the most requested and appears on their labels to this day.

EVAPORATED MILK VS.
SWEETENED CONDENSED MILK

UNDOUBTEDLY YOU'VE BAKED WITH EITHER sweetened condensed or evaporated milk, if not both. Perhaps one time you even mixed them up, yielding surprisingly delicious or possibly disappointing results. So what's the difference?

EVAPORATED MILK, which is also called dehydrated milk, is a shelf-stable product made from fresh milk with about 60 percent of the water removed. Evaporated milk has been used as a milk substitute in times of shortage; it was once believed that it was equally healthy for babies as breast milk (a theory since dismissed). Today, it's primarily used in baking, owing to its unique taste and keeping quality. Thanks to a series of back-of-the-label recipes, it became popular in homemade pumpkin pies; today, it is considered a key ingredient for the Thanksgiving dessert.

SWEETENED CONDENSED MILK is milk from which the water has been removed and to which sugar—lots of it—has been added. It's a very thick, sweet product that, when sealed in a can, can last for years without refrigeration. It gained popularity after being a prominent item in soldiers' rations during the Civil War, due to its high amount of protein and calories.

Pumpkin Pie

I DON'T SEE MUCH REASON TO FIX SOMETHING if it ain't broke, so this recipe reflects a traditional combination of ingredients. This version gets a decadent boost from using sweetened condensed milk. You'll greatly elevate the quality of this or any pie by making your own piecrust, preferably from a recipe that uses part or all butter (which helps create more flakes and more flavor). And to really put it over the top, use real maple syrup as the sweetener for your whipped cream accompaniment. Mmmm.

Makes one 9-inch pie (8 servings)

Dough for one 9-inch piecrust, homemade or store-bought

1½ teaspoons ground cinnamon

1 teaspoon ground ginger

¼ teaspoon ground cloves

1 teaspoon salt

2 large eggs

One 15-ounce can plain pumpkin purée

One 14-ounce can sweetened condensed milk

About 1 cup heavy cream, for serving (optional)

Granulated or powdered sugar (optional)

1. Position a rack in the center of the oven; preheat the oven to 425 degrees F.

2. Roll the pie dough into a circle about 12 inches in diameter; place it into the pie pan and crimp the edges (or use a commercial frozen pie shell). Keep the dough refrigerated while you prepare the filling.

3. In a small bowl, stir together the sugar, cinnamon, ginger, cloves, and salt. Set aside.

4. In a large bowl, beat the eggs; stir in the pumpkin and the sugar-and-spice mixture. Once well incorporated, stir in the sweetened condensed milk (it may incorporate better if you add the milk in 3 additions, ensuring that each addition is fully mixed in before adding the next).

5. Pour the filling into the prepared pie shell.

6. Bake for 15 minutes, then lower the oven temperature to 350 degrees F. Bake for an additional 40 to 45 minutes, or until a knife inserted into the center comes out clean. Cool on a wire rack to room temperature. Serve at room temperature, or refrigerate the pie and let it sit at room temperature for 30 minutes before serving.

7. Using an electric mixer or a large bowl with a balloon whisk, whip the cream until it forms very soft peaks. Add sugar to taste and whip a bit more, stopping before the cream becomes stiff and grainy. Top the pie slices with whipped cream.

LOST & FOUND

SOMETIMES DESSERTS ARE LOST OR FORGOTTEN. Over the years, tastes change, recipes adapt, and ingredients come into (and fall out of) vogue. Here's a collection of recipes that you don't often come across, but that have been rather influential and—even more importantly—continue to be delicious.

Baked Alaska

IT WOULDN'T BE SO CRAZY to assume that this dramatic dessert, characterized by a chilly core of ice cream with a thick coating of snowdrift-like meringue, hails from Alaska. But, alas, you'd be wrong. Baked Alaska may take its name from the Last Frontier, but it was born many miles away and many years prior to the state's annexation.

. . . .

The idea of cooking a cold dessert encased with pastry is documented as early as the 1700s in China. At that time, the desserts would have borne little resemblance to what we call Baked Alaska today—they would have been more like frozen ices or creams coated in breadcrumbs. However, when Chinese delegates introduced such treats to the French, the concept excited pastry chefs, who adapted it in a most delightful sugar-, cream-, and egg-filled way. America's first famous Francophile, Thomas Jefferson, may have served something along these lines as early as 1802.

But it's an eccentric genius named Count Rumford (born Benjamin Thompson) to whom we owe a big, sweet thanks when it comes to further developing this showy dessert—he's the one credited with introducing the meringue coating in the 1800s. Rumford was an interesting fellow—he was an American physicist living in Europe (and a former spy, to boot). Apparently in his free time he tinkered with food science—and while experimenting with dessert techniques, he realized that while pastry would conduct a lot of the heat and protect a cold core, a layer of meringue would do so to an even greater degree. He created a dessert that he called "omelette surprise," which was also dubbed *omelette à la norvégienne* or "Norwegian omelette," in reference to its snowy appearance.

The dessert's popularity caught on during the Victorian era, and these elaborate confections, often called *bombes*, were made in various fancy shapes.

The dessert's popularity caught on during the Victorian era, and these elaborate confections, often called bombes, were made in various fancy shapes.

In 1876, the dessert made a stateside splash at Delmonico's Restaurant in New York City, where Charles Ranhofer prepared it to celebrate the newly acquired Alaska Territory. Originally dubbed the "Alaska-Florida" (inspired by the cold-hot duality of the dessert), the name was eventually shortened to Baked Alaska. It became known as a dessert for the privileged, and was popularized in well-heeled destinations as far away as Monte Carlo.

After the blown-out bluster of the Victorian era and the dull austerity of the Depression and war years, the dessert enjoyed a renaissance in the 1950s, when Alaska was granted statehood. It was quite the popular hostess dessert and *piece de resistance* throughout the '60s. One flamboyant variation called Bombe Alaska calls for dark rum to be splashed over the Baked Alaska. Lights are then turned down and the whole dessert is flambéed while being served! Exercise caution if you decide to try this at home.

Baked Alaska

I'M WONDERING WHY TODAY'S RESTAURANT CHEFS haven't caught on to the cool retro-ness and sheer fun of Baked Alaska. But never mind—you can still make it, and it's definitely worth it: cold ice cream with toasty meringue makes for a delightful melding of flavors, temperatures, and textures. Thanks to Catherine McCord, founder of Weelicious.com, who shared the brownie base idea with me.

Makes one 9-inch dome (12 servings)

1. To make the ice cream dome, place a 3-quart mixing bowl (with a diameter of about 9 inches) in the freezer to chill. Line it with plastic wrap. Fill the bowl with ice cream; smooth and level the top surface. Cover the surface with plastic wrap and freeze until the ice cream is very hard, at least 4 hours, or up to 24 hours. Note: To make miniature Baked Alaskas, you can split the ice cream between multiple small domed bowls (with diameters of about 3 inches).

2. Set the brownie layer out on a large, flat, ovenproof plate. Unmold the ice cream dome on top of the brownie layer, but leave the plastic wrap on top. Trim any bottom edges of the brownie layer to make it flush with the ice cream. Place this big, cold blob into the freezer.

3. Make the meringue cover, then take the ice cream dome from the freezer and remove the plastic wrap. Spread the meringue onto the ice cream dome, covering it completely. Use the back of a spoon to flick and pull little peaks up from the surface (for a nubbly texture when it bakes). Freeze for at least 3 hours, or overnight.

4. Near the time you'd like to serve your Baked Alaska, heat the oven to 500 degrees F, making sure there's enough clearance to fit the dessert. When the oven is at temperature, remove the assembled *bombe* from the freezer, set it on a parchment-lined baking sheet, and put it into the oven. Bake for 3 to 5 minutes, rotating the dome once or twice, until the peaks turn a golden brown color. Let the cake stand at room temperature for about 15 minutes before serving (this will ensure that you'll be able to slice through it without the crust getting all gooey and oozey). Slice and serve; freeze any leftovers for up to 5 days.

10 cups (5 pint-size containers) ice cream, slightly softened (all one flavor, or several flavors)

Brownie Base (recipe follows)

6 cups Meringue Coating (recipe follows)

1 cup (2 sticks) unsalted
butter

8 ounces bittersweet chocolate, chopped (about 1 cup)

1 cup all-purpose flour

½ teaspoon baking powder

½ teaspoon salt

4 large eggs

2 cups sugar

2 teaspoons vanilla extract

BROWNIE BASE

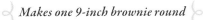

Makes one 9-inch brownie round

1. Heat the oven to 350 degrees F. Grease and flour the bottom and sides of a 9-inch round cake pan; line the bottom of the pan with parchment paper.

2. Heat the butter and chocolate over low heat, using either a small, heavy-bottomed saucepan or a double boiler. Stir occasionally until melted. Set aside to cool.

3. In a medium bowl, whisk the flour, baking powder, and salt until combined. Set aside.

4. In a large bowl, whisk the eggs, sugar, and vanilla until well combined. Add the slightly warm chocolate mixture to the eggs and whisk to combine. Add the flour mixture and stir with a wooden spoon until just combined. Spoon the batter into the prepared cake pan; use an offset or rubber spatula to smooth and level the batter.

5. Bake for 45 to 55 minutes, or until a toothpick inserted into the center comes out mostly clean. Set the pan on a wire rack until the brownie layer is completely cool.

8 egg whites, at room
temperature

¼ teaspoon cream of tartar

⅛ teaspoon salt

¾ cup sugar

MERINGUE COATING

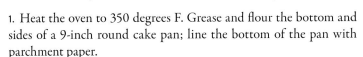

Makes about 6 cups meringue

1. Using a stand mixer with a clean, dry bowl and fitted with the whisk attachment, whip the egg whites, cream of tartar, and salt on medium-high speed until the whites form soft peaks. Increase the speed to high and add the sugar in a slow stream, continuing to whip until stiff, shiny peaks form.

Hermits

THE LATE 1800S WERE A PRETTY EVENTFUL TIME in the United States. The Statue of Liberty was installed; the Gold Rush began; motion pictures were invented; and the nation continued to grow, officially adding Washington, Montana, and the Dakotas to the Union. But what were our ancestors eating to keep their energy up during this busy time? According to *Betty Crocker's Cooky Book*, the cookie of the era was the hermit—a moist, fat, spicy cookie, rich with fruit and nuts. It originated in Cape Cod during the heyday of clipper ships, because it kept well on seafaring journeys.

. . . .

But where did this morsel get its funny name? There are a few theories. Some say that the cookies look like a hermit's brown sackcloth robe, but as charming an idea as that is, the argument seems weak: the cookies are sometimes pale, sometimes dark, and served in different shapes. And personally, even if I squint really hard and turn my head sideways, I still can't quite see the resemblance. A lead that sounds far more likely is that the recipe was derived from a spice cookie called the *hernhutter*, made by the Moravians, an ethnic group with a large community in Pennsylvania. This might have sounded like "hermits" to an English-speaking cook.

Funny name and hazy origins aside, there's definitely another reason why hermits have lingered in our cookie jars: they're rich, cakey, moist, and satisfying. They're also simple and wholesome, not unlike the initial settlers who likely baked them in New England kitchens. And true to their reputation as a seafaring cookie that kept for long periods of time without spoiling, these treats do store well—in fact, one 1886 recipe notes that the resulting cookies will "keep a century if not eaten."

Hermits

SOME PEOPLE SAY THAT THEY PREFER these cookies slightly dry or stale, which makes for good dunking with coffee or tea. But the choice is up to you—we don't often have to take long sea voyages anymore, and since this version includes eggs (the earliest recipes did not), it's probably best to enjoy them shortly after they come out of the oven. Adding raisins makes them taste vaguely virtuous, if you're into that—if you're not, chocolate chips work quite well, too.

Makes 3 dozen small or 2 dozen large cookies

1¾ cups all-purpose flour

½ teaspoon baking soda

½ teaspoon salt

½ teaspoon nutmeg

½ teaspoon cinnamon

⅛ teaspoon cloves

½ cup (1 stick) unsalted butter

¾ cup light brown sugar

¼ cup granulated sugar

1 large egg

¼ cup cold strong coffee

1 cup dark raisins (or substitute chocolate chips)

1 cup coarsely chopped nuts (your choice)

1. In a medium bowl, sift together the flour, baking soda, salt, nutmeg, cinnamon, and cloves. Set aside.

2. In a stand mixer fitted with the paddle attachment, mix the butter, brown sugar, and egg thoroughly. Add the coffee and mix to combine.

3. Add the flour, baking soda, salt, nutmeg, and cinnamon together in a large bowl. Add the mixture in 2 or 3 additions into the butter mixture, scraping the sides of the bowl with a rubber spatula as needed. Add the raisins and nuts and stir just until incorporated.

4. Chill the dough for at least 1 hour; this will ensure that the cookies do not spread as much. Preheat the oven to 400 degrees F and line 2 baking sheets with parchment paper.

5. If you want small cookies, drop rounded teaspoonfuls of dough onto the baking sheets; if you're not scared of a big cookie, use an ice cream scoop.

6. Bake for 8 to 10 minutes for small cookies and about 12 minutes for larger ones, or until there is the slightest crispiness on the bottom (as they have a light-brown hue from the coffee, you'll have to look carefully!). Transfer the cookies to a wire rack to cool. Store them at room temperature in an airtight container for up to 7 days.

Joe Froggers

JOE FROGGER: WHAT A JAUNTY NAME for a cookie! It conjures the image of a can-do cookie that will energize you with sugary goodness and make you "hop-to" the task at hand. But this chewy, spicy, saucer-sized molasses cookie's past is not quite as carefree and sweet as its name might imply.

. . . .

As the story goes, these famous molasses cookies were first made in Marblehead, Massachusetts, and took their name from the plump, dark little frogs that lived in a pond near the cottage of a fellow known as Uncle Joe. The cookies themselves are a balancing act: not too sweet, with a crisp texture, and quite large—the original versions were up to five inches in diameter. Like many cookies popular in that era, they also kept very well, owing to their lack of egg.

But who was this Uncle Joe? A little digging reveals the story of a life as rich as the cookie. Joe Brown, aka "Black Joe," was born in Massachusetts in 1750 to an African American mother and Native American father—a time when most wealthy Marblehead families still owned several slaves. He must have found employment or stayed under the radar, because his name does not appear as one of the "black drifters" forced out of town in 1788, when local government ordered all former slaves to find work or leave.

He ended up doing quite well for himself, and eventually married a woman more than twenty years his junior, Lucretia, who was nicknamed "Aunt Crese," or "Aunt Creesy." He even bought property in the area, a house on the aptly named Gingerbread Hill. It was a legendary spot in its time: the Browns converted it to a rooming house, and it was one of the few places in town where whites and blacks mixed freely. Joe would open up his tavern on a pretty regular basis—he'd play the fiddle, Aunt Crese would cook, and everyone would drink plenty of grog. And people ate, of course; the Browns were known for serving these salad plate–size cookies. According to Marblehead Historian Joseph Robinson, "a more uncouth assemblage of ruffians could not be found anywhere."

Joe Froggers

THESE COOKIES, LIKE THE STORY BEHIND THEM, will leave a lasting impression. Easy to make and pleasant to eat, these molasses-rich cookies, sparkling with a dusting of sugar, make a wonderfully spicy accompaniment to tea.

Makes 2 to 3 dozen large cookies

3¾ cups all-purpose flour, plus more for rolling

2 teaspoons salt

1 teaspoon baking soda

1¼ teaspoons ground ginger

½ teaspoon ground cloves

½ teaspoon ground nutmeg

½ cup (1 stick) unsalted butter, softened

1 cup sugar

1 cup dark molasses

½ cup water

Coarse sugar, for sprinkling the tops

1. In a medium bowl, stir together the flour, salt, ginger, baking soda, cloves, and nutmeg. Set to the side.

2. In a stand mixer fitted with the paddle attachment, cream the butter and sugar on high speed until light and fluffy, about 2 minutes, scraping down the bowl as needed with a rubber spatula. Reduce the speed to low and mix in the molasses and water.

3. In 2 or 3 increments, add the dry ingredients to the wet, mixing until completely combined. The dough will be dark and thick.

4. Scrape the dough from the bowl, flatten it into a disk, and wrap it tightly in plastic wrap; chill for at least 2 hours, or up to overnight.

5. When you're ready to bake the cookies, preheat the oven to 375 degrees F. Line 3 baking sheets with parchment paper. Set the wrapped dough out at room temperature for about 5 minutes to soften slightly so that it's easier to roll.

6. Sprinkle your work surface and the dough with flour; roll the dough to ¼ inch thick. Cut into approximately 3-inch circles, using a floured cookie cutter or the rim of a drinking glass. Sprinkle with coarse sugar. Place the circles on the prepared baking sheets, leaving about 1 inch around each one.

7. Bake for 10 to 12 minutes, or until the cookies have a dull finish on top. Let them cool on the baking sheet for a few minutes before transferring to a wire rack to cool completely. Store the cookies in an airtight container at room temperature for up to 7 days, or in airtight bags in the freezer for up to 2 months.

Jumbles

WHEN I PONDER THE LONG AND ARDUOUS JOURNEY the pilgrims made from Europe to the New World, one question rises in my mind above all others: what did they eat for dessert? Well, this wasn't a period known for its excess of dessert options. However, if travelers of that era *were* to be eating cookies, they'd probably be jumbles. Never heard of a Jumble? I'm not surprised, but you've certainly heard of the cookies that are its direct descendants, such as sugar cookies and snickerdoodles.

. . . .

Jumbles are cookies originally documented in Europe as early as the sixteenth century. Strictly speaking, they weren't really a remarkable cookie. In the earliest versions, they're little more than sweetened flour and water. But since they kept basically forever and fared well on long voyages, they were one of the first cookies to travel, period—and therefore, one of the first cookies to find their way over to the New World.

Shaping was a hallmark of the cookie: even early American recipes specify that the dough be shaped into rings, and hostesses would create more elaborate shapes—often figure eights—for company. Incidentally, this also may explain the name Jumble, which is derived from *gemel*, meaning "twin" in Latin—like the twin loops of a figure eight. Some say that these open shapes made them easier to eat, as they tended to harden up during those long sitting periods. (Perhaps they were rock-like, but still, I'd rather eat a sweet little rock than hardtack any day of the week.) Today's jumbles are usually baked as drop cookies rather than in the original cut-and-formed style.

Now, I realize that I have perhaps not given the Jumble the hardest sell as a delicious morsel. But here's the thing: Jumbles have come a long way since those earliest days. True, they're still a humble cookie at heart; maybe it's best to consider the basic recipe as a simple but sturdy blank canvas—and to appreciate them for just that.

Jumbles

ONE OF THE BEST THINGS ABOUT THIS RECIPE is that it's exceedingly easy to make. This Jumble is updated from the earliest versions, but is still satisfyingly old-fashioned, yielding a soft, pillowy cookie that's spicy and only lightly sweet. Coarsely chopped pecans add a pleasing richness and slight crunch. And while they're wonderful as is, tailor them to your taste preferences with spices, different nuts, or frosting!

Makes 2 dozen cookies

2 cups all-purpose flour

½ teaspoon baking soda

½ teaspoon salt

½ cup (1 stick) unsalted butter, softened

1 cup sugar

1 large egg

¾ cup half-and-half

1 teaspoon vanilla extract

½ cup coarsely chopped pecans (optional)

1. Sift the flour, baking soda, and salt together in a large bowl until well combined; set aside.

2. In a stand mixer fitted with the paddle attachment, cream the butter and sugar on medium-high speed until very light and fluffy, 3 to 5 minutes. Add the egg and mix until fully incorporated. Add the half-and-half and vanilla and mix to combine.

3. Add the flour mixture in 2 or 3 increments, mixing well with each addition, until fully incorporated. If you're using nuts, add them now and mix gently, just until incorporated. Cover the dough and refrigerate it for about 1 hour.

4. Preheat the oven to 400 degrees F. Lightly grease 2 baking sheets.

5. Using a teaspoon or a mini ice cream scoop, drop rounds of dough on the baking sheets, leaving at least 2 inches around each dough ball.

6. Bake for 8 to 10 minutes. The cookies will not be brown on top, but will have a slight toasty color on the bottom. Allow them to cool on the baking sheets for a few minutes, then use a metal spatula to transfer them to a wire rack and finish cooling. Store the cookies at room temperature in an airtight container; they'll keep for up to 5 days.

SWEET CELEBRITIES: BAKED GOODS NAMED AFTER PEOPLE

SARAH BERNHARDT CAKES: Is it a cookie? Is it a cake? Regardless, this tasty, small, nutty, meringue-like pastry covered with chocolate takes its name from French stage (and early film) actress Sarah Bernhardt.

CHARLOTTE RUSSE: This cold dessert of Bavarian cream is set in a mold lined with ladyfingers; it was invented by the French chef Marie-Antoine Carême, who named either it in honor of his Russian employer Czar Alexander I (Russe being French for Russian) or Queen Charlotte of the United Kingdom.

FRANGIPANE: This almond pastry filling and tart was named for Marquis Muzio Frangipani, a sixteenth-century Italian botanist who developed a well-known bitter-almond-scented perfume.

LAMINGTONS: This popular Australian dessert consists of a small square of white cake (sponge, butter, or pound) that is dipped in a sweet chocolate icing and then coated in desiccated coconut. I suspect Lord Lamington (Governor of Queensland from 1896 to 1901) might be surprised at how popular these cakes have become.

NESSELRODE PUDDING (AND NESSELRODE PIE): This chestnut-rich confection (sometimes secretly supplemented with pureed cauliflower!) takes its name from Russian diplomat Count Karl Robert von Nesselrode. As a pie, Nesselrode enjoyed a vogue in the New York area in the 1950s, but has all but disappeared.

RIGÓ JANCSI: This Viennese cube-shaped chocolate sponge cake and cream pastry is named after the famous Gypsy violinist, Rigó Jancsi (by Hungarian tradition, Rigó is his last name, Jancsi his first—the name literally means Johnny Blackbird).

SAVARIN: This is a yeast-raised sweet cake soaked in Kirsch or rum that restaurant pastry chefs still revere and put on their menus today. It's named for the legendary chef Brillat-Savarin, considered by some the first *real* gastronome, author of *The Physiology of Taste*, and a documented cheese lover who once said "A dessert without cheese is like a beautiful woman with only one eye."

Tunnel of Fudge Cake

NO IFS, ANDS, OR BUNDTS: this is one highly influential cake. Before individual molten chocolate cakes became ubiquitous on every fancy restaurant menu, before Bundt cake pans proliferated in cookery stores, there was the Tunnel of Fudge Cake, a crispy-crusted cake with an ooey-gooey, fudge-like interior.

. . . .

But the Tunnel would not have funneled into our everyday parlance without the invention of the Bundt pan, which preceded the recipe by several years. The Bundt pan was developed in the 1950s by H. David Dalquist, who had quite an eclectic career, working as a metallurgical engineer and a radar technician before starting a specialty cookware company that manufactured Nordic Ware. The pan's unique design was inspired by a traditional ceramic dish with a similar ringed shape. Though Dalquist's version was lighter and easier to use than the clunky previous version, sales were underwhelming.

Until 1966, that is, when Ella Helfrich came along and entered her recipe for Tunnel of Fudge Cake in the Pillsbury Bake-Off. In case you're not familiar with the Bake-Off, it's probably America's most famous baking contest, in which a hundred finalists are assembled in one spot to bake their finest recipes featuring Pillsbury products. They vie for some seriously sweet prizes: in 1966, the grand prize was $50,000 (today that would equate to a cool $1 million).

Helfrich was no novice to the Bake-Off—she had entered recipes for twelve consecutive years. All her hard work paid off in '66—her "Tunnel of Fudge" cake took second place, winning her a respectable $5,000 in prize money.

Although the recipe wasn't the grand prizewinner (that year, the honor went to a yeasted snack bread made with flour, cream cheese, and dry onion soup mix)—Ella's cake was clearly the darling of the public eye. Assembled in mere minutes by—here's the really groundbreaking part—mixing packaged frosting into a typical cake batter, the resulting cake was characterized by a chewy, brownie-edge-type exterior that gave way to a softer, chocolaty fudge-and-nut filling not unlike a decadent brownie batter.

The cake was an overnight sensation, and as a result, so was the Bundt pan; Pillsbury was immediately swamped with more than 200,000 requests for the pan, and Dalquist's company went into overtime production. Today, more than 50 million Bundt pans have been sold around the world. Seriously, just thinking of the day that the orders started pouring in to the Nordic Ware factory seems like the bakeware equivalent of the scene when all those letters are delivered to Santa in *Miracle on 34th Street.*

The cake was an overnight sensation, and as a result, so was the Bundt pan; Pillsbury was immediately swamped with more than 200,000 requests for the pan.

With more and more Bundt pans in the world, making the cake was easier than ever—but there was yet another twist in the road. At a certain point Pillsbury stopped production of a key ingredient in the cake: the Double Dutch Cocoa frosting mix. This was big bad news to avid home bakers who had fallen deeply in love with the Tunnel of Fudge Cake. Thankfully, in response to public demand, the Pillsbury test kitchens developed a from-scratch version of the recipe, which I've adapted here.

It seems no coincidence that not that long after the cake's initial popularity, a slurry of similar concoctions began working their way onto restaurant dessert menus. So next time you're out enjoying a molten or lava cake, you can thank Ella Helfrich for paving the way.

Tunnel of Fudge Cake

I CAN'T THINK OF A SINGLE REASON why you wouldn't want to taste the legend itself by making your very own Tunnel of Fudge Cake to enjoy at home! You'll be so glad you did. Pillsbury was so kind as to share this recipe with me. For the best results, use a Bundt-type or fluted cake pan, and don't cut corners on the nuts—if you don't use the amount specified, it doesn't quite work.

 Makes one 10-inch Bundt cake (12 servings)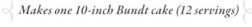

1. Preheat the oven to 350 degrees F. Grease and flour a 10-inch Bundt pan, making sure to get into all the nooks and crannies of the pan.

2. In the bowl of a stand mixer fitted with the paddle attachment, combine the sugar and butter; beat on medium-high speed until light and fluffy, 3 to 5 minutes.

3. Add the eggs one at a time, beating well after each addition and pausing to scrape the sides of the bowl with a rubber spatula as needed.

4. Gradually add the confectioners' sugar; blend well. Remove the bowl from the mixer.

5. Sift the flour with the cocoa powder; add this mixture, about 1 cup at a time, to the batter. Stir it by hand, using a wooden spoon, until the dry ingredients are just combined. Add the nuts and stir until well blended.

6. Spoon the batter into the prepared pan; spread evenly, leveling the top with an offset or rubber spatula.

7. Bake for 45 to 50 minutes, or until top is set and edges are beginning to pull away from sides of pan (a cake tester or toothpick inserted into the center of the cake will still be gooey).

8. Cool upright in the pan on a wire rack until just slightly warm, about 1½ hours. Invert onto a serving plate; cool for at least 2 hours more (this will allow the filling to set).

9. Spoon the glaze over the top of cake, allowing some to run down the sides. Store in the refrigerator, tightly covered, for up to 3 days. Let come to room temperature before serving.

1¾ cups granulated sugar

1¾ cups unsalted butter, softened

6 large eggs

2 cups confectioners' sugar

2¼ cups Pillsbury BEST® All Purpose or Unbleached Flour

¾ cup unsweetened cocoa powder

2 cups toasted chopped nuts (walnuts, pecans, or hazelnuts all work nicely)

½ cup Thick Chocolate Glaze (recipe follows)

¾ cup confectioners' sugar

¼ cup unsweetened cocoa powder

1½ to 2 tablespoons whole or 2% milk

THICK CHOCOLATE GLAZE

 Makes about ½ cup glaze

1. Sift together the sugar and cocoa.

1. Combine all of the ingredients in a small bowl, adding just enough milk for your desired drizzling consistency.

Wellesley Fudge Cake

A DEEPLY INDULGENT CHOCOLATE CAKE topped with a slab of thick fudge frosting, the likes of which will stick to your front teeth in the most pleasing way—seems an unlikely sweet to associate with the prim-and-proper ladies of renowned Wellesley College, founded in 1870 outside of Boston. But it seems that those young ladies had as voracious an appetite for the sweet stuff as they did for knowledge.

. . . .

Let's rewind a little bit, to the invention of fudge itself. Fudge, that smooth, semisoft candy made of butter, sugar, and various flavorings, is an Americanized version of French bonbons and creams, and it became popular in the United States in the early 1900s. But why the association with women's colleges?

Well, the young ladies at Wellseley (despite being expressly bound by an official college rule "neither to buy nor receive in any manner whatsoever any confectionery or eatables of any kind not provided for them by the College") would use the sweet stuff as their excuse to stay up late; making the candy themselves was something of a loophole. "Nearly every night at college," said one student, "some girl may be found somewhere who is making 'fudges' or giving a fudge party." By 1908 the term was commonly used in association with women's colleges. A 1909 cookbook produced by Walter Baker & Co. (producer of Baker's Chocolate) includes three different recipes for fudge, all named after the three most prestigious women's schools: Vassar, Smith, and Wellesley.

In fact, there's a letter in the Vassar archives that I present as proof of how widespread fudge-making was in ladies' colleges. It reads: "Fudge, as I first knew it, was first made in Baltimore by a cousin of a schoolmate of

> "Nearly every night at college," said one student, "some girl may be found somewhere who is making 'fudges' or giving a fudge party." By 1908 the term was commonly used in association with women's colleges.

mine. It was sold in 1886 in a grocery store . . . . I secured a recipe and in my first year at Vassar, I made it there—and in 1888 I made 30 pounds for the Senior auction, its real introduction to the college, I think." By 1913, fudge and fudge cakes were common on the tearoom menus surrounding the college.

Wellesley Fudge Cake

SOME OLDER RECIPES ARE UNFROSTED; others, like this one, feature a double dose of chocolate, the base of which is like a cakey brownie, coated with a thick, fudge-like frosting. And while the cake does require a bit of candy-making prowess, it is astoundingly easy to eat. Don't have buttermilk? Don't worry; this is easily attained by adding one tablespoon of lemon juice to one cup of milk. It will curdle rapidly but will taste great when mixed and baked, that's a promise.

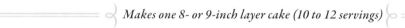

Makes one 8- or 9-inch layer cake (10 to 12 servings)

1. Position a rack in the center of the oven; preheat the oven to 350 degrees F. Grease and flour 2 round 8- or 9-inch cake pans; line the bottoms with parchment paper.

2. Sift the flour, baking soda, and salt in a large bowl. Set aside.

3. In a small saucepan over medium heat, bring the water, chocolate, and ½ cup of the granulated sugar to a simmer, stirring constantly until the mixture has melted. Remove from the heat and cool until lukewarm.

4. In the bowl of an electric mixer fitted with the paddle attachment, cream the butter and remaining granulated sugar on medium-high speed until light and fluffy, 3 to 5 minutes.

5. Reduce speed to low and beat in the eggs, one at a time, until incorporated, pausing to scrape down the sides of the bowl between additions. Beat in the vanilla.

6. Reduce the mixer speed to low and add the chocolate mixture to the butter mixture and beat until fully incorporated.

7. Continuing on low speed, add the flour mixture alternately with the buttermilk, in 2 to 3 additions each, ensuring that each addition is fully mixed in before adding the next. Scrape down the sides of the bowl with a rubber spatula after each addition.

8. Divide the batter equally between the 2 pans, using an offset or rubber spatula to smooth and level the batter. Lift the pans and let fall onto the counter to ensure one last spread to settle the batter.

2¼ cups all-purpose flour

1 teaspoon baking soda

1 teaspoon salt

½ cup hot water

4 ounces unsweetened baking chocolate, chopped into pieces (about ¾ cup)

1¼ cups granulated sugar, divided

¾ cup unsalted butter, softened

½ cup lightly packed light brown sugar

3 large eggs

⅔ cup buttermilk

1 teaspoon vanilla extract

2½ cups Wellesley Fudge Frosting (recipe follows)

9. Bake the cakes for 25 to 30 minutes, rotating the pans halfway through the baking time. A toothpick inserted into the center should come out mostly clean. (It will be difficult to detect doneness by the color of the cake, as it will be quite dark.)

10. Let the cakes cool for about 10 minutes. Run a small knife around the edges of the cakes to loosen the sides, then flip them out onto a wire rack. Peel off the parchment paper, turn the cakes right side up, and let them cool completely. If the cakes have formed domes during baking, level them by using a large serrated knife before frosting.

11. To assemble the cake, place one cake on a serving platter. Use about ¾ cup of the frosting and spread it evenly over the layer. Place the second cake layer on top. The weight of the top layer will cause the frosting to spread.

12. Generously frost the sides and top of the cake. Serve in large wedges. The cake will keep, covered, at cool room temperature for about 3 days.

WELLESLEY FUDGE FROSTING

 Makes about 2½ cups frosting

8 ounces unsweetened chocolate, finely chopped (about 1 cup)

½ cup (1 stick) unsalted butter, softened

Dash of salt

½ cup evaporated milk

1 teaspoon vanilla extract

4 to 5 cups confectioners' sugar, sifted

Whole or 2% milk or cream (optional)

1. In a large saucepan over low heat, melt the chocolate and butter, stirring frequently until smooth and melted. Remove from the heat.

1. Add the salt, evaporated milk, and vanilla; stir until smooth. Let cool to lukewarm, stirring occasionally.

1. Gradually stir in the sugar, cup by cup, until an ideal spreading consistency has been reached. (You may not need all of the sugar). If needed, add a small quantity of milk to thin the frosting.

FOREIGN AFFAIRS

TRAVEL SPEAKS TO OUR SENSE OF ADVENTURE, curiosity, and romance. It piques our imagination and induces daydreams. After all, who wouldn't love to take a moonlit stroll along the Seine, to explore the narrow streets of Vienna, to traipse along the outback of Australia—or at the very least see in what direction the toilets flush on the other hemisphere?

While physical travel might not always be within our means, desserts that originated on foreign soil provide an opportunity to get a delicious taste of different cultures—and in this case, to hear some interesting stories too.

ANZAC Biscuits

TO CUT RIGHT TO THE CHASE: ANZAC biscuits are a simple, crispy cookie made using oats, flour, coconut, butter, and golden syrup (I know you were wondering). It wouldn't be hard to imagine them in the role of the oatmeal cookie's crunchier, coconut-studded cousin. But their humble appearance should not imply that their story lacks dimension or complexity.

. . . .

To begin with, the funny name: What does ANZAC mean? ANZAC is an acronym for Australian and New Zealand Army Corps. But why name a cookie ("biscuit," down under) after the armed forces? Well, because this biscuit's starring role in the culinary world began in the era of World War I, when wives and girlfriends would send them to their fellows in the army because they were easy-to-stock items that wouldn't spoil in transit.

During the war, in a surge of patriotic pride, many recipes both sweet and savory were labeled ANZAC: think ANZAC casserole, ANZAC sandwiches, and the like. But after the war, the name stuck with these cookies in particular. Perhaps it's because the biscuits were somewhat similar to an item that was regularly featured in soldiers' rations, called ANZAC Tile—a sort of hardtack that I'd warrant probably tasted about as good as it sounds. The cookie-like version has remained in heavy rotation ever since; throughout Australia and New Zealand, it's ubiquitous in coffee shops, bakeries, and as a prepackaged snack item.

This biscuit's starring role in the culinary world began in the era of World War I, when wives and girlfriends would send them to their fellows in the army because they were easy-to-stock items that wouldn't spoil in transit.

But while Australia and New Zealand are quite content with sharing their armed forces, they're not quite so nice about sharing this baked good: both locations insist that they invented the biscuit. This isn't the first time they've butted heads over the lineage of a baked good, however: they also fought over the origin of Pavlova, an angel-light meringue dessert (New Zealand ultimately won). However, determining who "owns" the ANZAC is a bit more difficult. While they're largely considered Australia's National Biscuit, it's possible that they evolved from Scottish oatcakes, which gained popularity in New Zealand following the arrival of a large Scottish immigrant population in the nineteenth and twentieth centuries.

In Australia, however, a certain level of authenticity is demanded of these biscuits. "ANZAC" is protected by Australian law, and misuse can be cause for legal action. In 1994 they adopted a general policy to allow the common usage of the name "ANZAC biscuit," but warned that it had better be used properly. The official government policy reads as follows:

"It should be noted that approvals for the word 'ANZAC' to be used on biscuit products have been given provided that the product generally conforms to the traditional recipe and shape, and is not used in association with the word 'cookies,' with its non-Australian overtones. For instance, an application for ANZAC biscuits dipped in chocolate would not be approved as they would not conform with the traditional recipe." *Well.*

And they're not fooling around: In 2008, the international chain Subway began selling something called ANZAC Biscuits, but they were not made following the original recipe. Deemed inauthentic, the Department of Veterans Affairs demanded that for Subway to continue selling them, they'd have to adhere to the original recipe. Subway declined on the grounds that it was too hard to duplicate the recipe in a cost-effective way.

Following is a recipe that will please people on all continents. They still ship well, too.

ANZAC Biscuits

ONE OF THE KEY INGREDIENTS IN THIS RECIPE is golden syrup, a thick, sugar-based liquid with a color and flavor somewhat similar to honey. If you can't find golden syrup, substitute one tablespoon of Karo syrup plus one-and-a-half teaspoons maple syrup or light molasses. Or take a little shopping excursion to England, Australia, or New Zealand, where you'll find it in nearly every neighborhood market!

Makes 3 dozen cookies

1 cup all-purpose flour

1 cup sugar

1 cup old-fashioned rolled oats

1 cup unsweetened desiccated or dried coconut

½ cup (1 stick) unsalted butter

1 tablespoon golden syrup, such as Lyle's (available at specialty grocery stores)

2 tablespoons boiling water, plus 1 to 2 tablespoons more as needed

1 teaspoon baking soda

1. Preheat the oven to 375 degrees F. Line 2 baking sheets with parchment paper and set aside.

2. In a large bowl, stir together the flour, sugar, oats, and coconut until well mixed.

3. In a small saucepan, melt the butter and golden syrup over medium heat, stirring occasionally.

4. In a small bowl, combine the boiling water and baking soda, stirring until the baking soda dissolves. Stir into the butter mixture. Enjoy watching the bubbly reaction!

5. Transfer the butter mixture to a large bowl, or to the bowl of a stand mixer fitted with the paddle attachment. Add the dry ingredients, mixing until fully incorporated. If the dough seems overly dry or stiff, add another tablespoon or two of hot water.

6. Drop the batter by heaping teaspoonfuls onto the prepared baking sheet; leave 1 inch around each biscuit to allow for spreading. Bake for 12 minutes, or until golden brown.

7. Remove from the oven; allow the biscuits to cool on the tray for a few minutes before transferring them to a wire rack to cool completely. These biscuits will keep well for up to 2 weeks stored in an airtight container at room temperature.

Cherries Jubilee

WHEN IT COMES TO FLAMING DESSERTS, Bananas Foster gets the biggest blaze of glory, but really, this bananarama might not even exist were it not for a dish called cherries jubilee, as jubilant a dessert as there ever was. It's a beautiful concoction of deep red cherries heated with liqueur, which is flambéed and served as a warm, syrup-like sauce over vanilla ice cream. A show like that kind of puts hot fudge to shame, don't you think?

. . . .

Cherries jubilee is credited to Auguste Escoffier, a sort of culinary superstar of the late nineteenth and early twentieth centuries who, to list a few bullet points on his resume, is credited as the father of modern canning, the inventor of the first à la carte menu, and a revolutionary for paring down and streamlining the modern restaurant kitchen. Though he had a knack for simplification, cherries jubilee is proof that he clearly wasn't averse to a bit of flashiness.

To set the stage for the invention of cherries jubilee: it's 1887. Queen Victoria is visiting the French Riviera to celebrate the fiftieth year of her reign, also referred to as her Golden Jubilee. Escoffier is *chef de cuisine* at the Grand Hotel in Monte Carlo. Cue the party planner: Victoria's son, the Prince of Wales, knows that Escoffier is the go-to guy in the area for fancy food. Armed with the knowledge that Victoria is very fond of cherries, he hires Escoffier to create a dish suiting the occasion. Everyone loves it! Then, like now, the goings-on of royalty were of great interest to the public, and cherries jubilee was widely celebrated and embraced.

Original recipes call for syrup-poached sweet cherries to be poured into fireproof dishes, then combined with warm brandy and set aflame at the moment of serving. Oddly, the one thing that is missing from many versions of the recipe is the

Then, like now, the goings-on of royalty were of great interest to the public, and cherries jubilee was widely celebrated and embraced.

accompaniment of ice cream. It's possible that originally the dish was meant as a more all-purpose dessert sauce, but soon after its invention, the recipe was being served to dignitaries as a delicious ice cream topping. So it seems that even if not the original intent, serving the dish in this manner quickly became the favored delivery system.

Of course, it's fun to ponder whether the ice cream omission was intentional, as suggested in the somewhat racy historical novel inspired by Escoffier, entitled *White Truffles in Winter*. The story says that the Queen found such a sensual pleasure in the cherries alone that any accompaniment would be an "insult" to the decadent dish.

Following the invention of Bananas Foster in 1951 by Chef Paul Blangé (at the legendary Brennan's Restaurant in Louisiana), flaming sweets enjoyed a period of popularity as a flashy dinner-party and restaurant dessert. For the cherry-averse, other variations were available: Mangos Diablo (mangos flambéed in tequila) and Pêches Louis (peaches flamed in whiskey), and of course, Crêpes Suzette. Though not as popular in restaurants today as they were in years past, these dishes remain an easy and extremely fun way to entertain and delight party guests. But please, do not set yourself on fire.

Cherries Jubilee

AT YOUR NEXT DINNER PARTY, why not try this ultra-simple combination of sweet syrup-like sauce drizzled over classic vanilla ice cream? If you want to get a little creative, you could try different flavors of ice cream—dark chocolate might be amazing, or maybe lemon. Add a buttery shortbread cookie or wafer on the side and you'll have created a dessert that your friends will be talking about for a long time.

 *Makes 6 servings*

1. Drain the cherries, reserving the juice.

2. In a large sauté pan over medium heat, combine the cherry juice, sugar, and cornstarch; stir occasionally, until the sugar has dissolved and the mixture begins to thicken, about 5 minutes. Add the butter and stir until completely incorporated. Add the cherries to the pan and stir gently until warmed.

3. Bring the mixture to a boil and add the alcohol of your choice. Using a long-handled match and leaning back from the pan, set the mixture aflame. It will go out on its own in a few moments; once it does, serve immediately on top of 6 bowls of ice cream.

One 15- or 16-ounce can pitted black cherries in juice

2 tablespoons sugar

1½ teaspoons cornstarch

2 tablespoons unsalted butter, cut into ½-inch pieces, softened

¼ cup kirsch, cognac, or brandy

2 pints vanilla ice cream

Croissants

AH, THE CROISSANT. Could there possibly be a Frenchier thing on the planet than these crescents of delectable, flaky butter pastry, lightly crunchy on the outside, ethereally soft on the inside? You might not think so, but here's a curious fact: while certainly most strongly associated with France, they are really an Austrian creation.

. . . .

There are several colorful tales surrounding the origins of the croissant, including one that celebrates Austrian bakers for foiling a plot by the Turks during a war between the two countries, and one that credits Marie Antoinette herself with bringing the treats to Paris from her native Austria. Unfortunately, as delightful as these stories are, they're simply not true. So how did it really go down?

Croissants were preceded by something called *kipferl*, or "pointed little loaves of white bread," a sort of dowdier, simpler version of the croissant that hailed from Austria. (If you want to get really technical about it, crescent-shaped breads preceded even Austria, where in ancient Greece, moon-shaped cakes were considered offerings to the Gods—but for now we'll stick to kipferl.) The birth of the croissant itself dates to the mid-1800s, when an Austrian artillery officer, August Zang, founded a Viennese bakery (cleverly named Boulangerie Viennoise) in Paris.

Importantly, Zang is credited with introducing yeast into the butter pastry form, and his methods quickly took off. The pastry began to resemble what we know today, and it was named *croissant* for its crescent shape. The croissant was adopted by the French: production took off, and the word quickly entered the everyday vocabulary. In the 1860s, it was recognized in esteemed

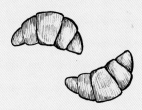

Could there possibly be a Frenchier thing on the planet than these crescents of delectable, flaky butter pastry, lightly crunchy on the outside, ethereally soft on the inside?

French dictionary *Littre*, and in 1872, Charles Dickens even mentioned it in one of his articles—at the time, sort of like hitting the pop-culture jackpot for pastry.

Today, the image of the croissant has firmly attached itself to France, and with good reason: while perhaps it was not born there, it spent its formative years and truly came into its own there. Many of the flavor variations we now consider classic were developed in France, too. One is the *croissant aux amandes*, or "almond croissant"—the cleverest use of day-old bread ever: a croissant split, filled with almond cream, and baked again. The *pain au chocolat*, or "chocolate croissant," is another. *Merci, merci.*

Croissants

MAKING YOUR OWN CROISSANTS is something you should do at least once in your life! The resulting moon-shaped shards of pure pastry pleasure will leave you feeling almost absurdly accomplished and brimming with pride at your pastry prowess (and probably covered with flour and butter). Note: Not only will you want to clear out some time in your schedule to make these, but to make your life easier, also have ready a nonstick mat, a ruler, and plenty of counter space. Huge thanks to Jennifer Lee of Jen7714.wordpress.com, who kindly let me use her croissant method.

Makes 12 croissants

3½ cups all-purpose flour, divided

1 cup warm water

1 teaspoon active dry yeast

¼ cup whole or 2% milk

½ tablespoon unsalted butter, melted

1 teaspoon salt

1¾ cups (14 ounces) cold unsalted butter

1 large egg plus 1 tablespoon water, for egg wash

1. In a large bowl, mix 1 cup of the flour with the water and yeast, just until the flour is incorporated. Set the bowl aside; let the dough rise for 1 hour.

2. Add the remaining 2½ cups flour, milk, melted butter, and salt. Gently knead the mixture for about 1 minute to combine the ingredients. Cover the bowl with a clean, moist towel and let sit for about 20 minutes.

3. Now it is time to knead the dough in earnest. In the bowl of an electric mixer fitted with the dough hook, knead the dough on low speed for 15 to 20 minutes, or until the dough is smooth and elastic. This can also be done by hand, kneading more vigorously for about 10 minutes. Wrap the dough in plastic wrap. Refrigerate for 30 minutes.

4. Place the cold butter between 2 pieces of plastic wrap. Using a rolling pin, pound the butter into an 8-inch square (measure it—it matters).

5. Remove the dough from the refrigerator. On a lightly floured surface, roll the dough into a 9-by-17-inch rectangle. Gently place the square of butter on the bottom half of the rectangle, leaving just a small margin around the bottom edge of the dough. The butter should not be so soft that you cannot transfer it; if it is, return it to the refrigerator for a few minutes.

6. Fold the top half of the dough rectangle down over the bottom half, so that the butter is completely enclosed. Press together the

edges of the dough, forming a seal. Using your hands, even out the dough so that it is a fairly neat rectangle.

7. Using a rolling pin, gently roll the dough (you don't want the butter to pop out!) until it has formed a new rectangle about 9 by 18 inches. Once again, these measurements matter.

8. Fold the dough rectangle into thirds, like you would a letter going in an envelope: Orient the rectangle like a sheet of paper and begin folding the bottom third up toward the middle. Then fold the top third down. Remember this step, because you're going to have to do it again.

9. Align the dough so that if you pictured it as a book, the "spine" is to the left. Now, you are going to repeat the rolling and folding steps. Roll out the dough into another 9-by-18-inch rectangle. Repeat the process in the previous step (folding into the thirds with the top and bottom). Make a mental note: You've made 2 folds.

10. Wrap the dough in plastic wrap. Refrigerate for at least 1 hour.

11. Remove the dough from the refrigerator and repeat the folding process again, 2 more times. Repeat the refrigeration between foldings. Make a mental note: Now you're up to 4 folds.

12. I know that you're getting bored, but stay with me, because the dough is ready to be rolled out and shaped. If you're tired, though, you can wrap the dough and refrigerate again for several hours, or up to overnight.

13. Line 2 baking sheets with parchment paper and set aside.

14. Remove the dough from the refrigerator. Cut the dough in half. Return one half to the refrigerator while you work with the other.

15. On a lightly floured surface, roll one half of the dough into a 6½-by-20-inch rectangle, about ¼ inch thick. Place on one of the prepared baking sheets. Repeat this step with the second half of the dough. Let the dough chill, right on the sheet, for about 30 minutes.

16. Remove one of the trays from the refrigerator. Using a knife, cut the dough into 3 equal parts along the same imaginary "folds" as when rolling the dough. Cut each rectangle diagonally into 2

triangles. You should end up with 6 triangles. Repeat with the second tray of dough.

17. Make a small vertical slit in the middle of the base of each triangle. This allows you to roll the triangles into a crescent shape: Using both hands, roll each triangle into a crescent starting from the base. Tuck the tip of the triangle on the bottom (this will keep them from unrolling while baking).

18. Place the croissants back on the prepared baking sheets. Cover them with plastic wrap or a wet paper towel to "proof" for 1 hour at room temperature.

19. Position 2 racks in the center of the oven; preheat the oven to 375 degrees F. Line 2 baking sheets with parchment paper and set aside.

20. Apply the egg wash directly before baking.

21. Place the trays in the oven. Bake for 25 to 30 minutes, rotating the trays halfway through baking, or until the croissants have puffed and turned golden. Let cool on the trays before transferring to a wire rack to cool completely.

Gingerbread Men

REALLY, HE'S THE PERFECT MAN. He's tall, dark, and handsome. He smells nice. He's quiet but not brooding. And when you get tired of him, it's totally OK to bite his head off. And then eat the rest of him, too. We're talking, of course, about the spicy cut-out cookie known as the Gingerbread Man, a tasty holiday classic, famously personified in a classic children's story, and immortalized by his famous line, "Run, run, as fast as you can! Can't catch me, I'm the Gingerbread Man!" Well, perhaps it's time to chase down the tale of how this well-*bread* (pun intended) fellow came to be so famous.

. . . .

As it turns out, the Gingerbread Man carries a serious pastry pedigree. Gingerbread itself is very, very old—it was a tradition that began in Europe not long after ginger's entry to the continent in the year 992. The spice wasn't merely flavorful, it also acted as a natural preservative—and in addition to being used to mask the scent of decaying meat, the spice became a frequent addition to bread recipes. Fairly early in the game, bakers cut the bread into shapes and decorated them with sugar. By the 1600s, the bread, since dubbed *Lebkuchen*, or "cake of life," was so respected that in Germany and France only professional gingerbread bakers were allowed to bake the spicy treat. Thankfully, rules relaxed during Christmas and Easter, when anyone was permitted to do so. Nuremberg, Germany, became known as the Gingerbread Capital of the World when the bakers' guild employed master bakers and artisans to create intricate works of art from gingerbread.

A tasty holiday classic, famously personified in a classic children's story, and immortalized by his famous line, "Run, run, as fast as you can! Can't catch me, I'm the Gingerbread Man!"

We have England to thank for man-shaped gingerbread cookies. In the sixteenth century, the English adopted and revamped the recipe a bit by adding eggs and sweeteners, the result being a lighter and more delicate product.

Gingerbread men were first presented by Queen Elizabeth I, who definitely made a sweet impression on visiting dignitaries by presenting them with gingerbread characters baked in their own likenesses.

That first batch of delicious gingerbread men had its effect, and the custom caught on; when the English immigrated to America, these sweet fellows came along for the ride. "Shape [the dough] to your fancy," Amelia Simmons recommended to housewives in *American Cookery*, the first published American cookbook. Entrepreneurial peddlers picked up on the trend and started selling fancifully shaped tin cookie cutters. In Pennsylvania Dutch country, gingerbread men and ladies measuring more than a foot high, iced with buttons and smiles, were used to festively decorate windows during the holidays, making chilly passers-by smile. Of course, this is a good indication of why the tradition continues: these cookies are extremely effective at a most important task, which is making people happy.

But doesn't every gingerbread man need a place to hang his hat? The tradition of baking sweetly decorated gingerbread houses began in Germany after the Brothers Grimm published their collection of German fairy tales in the early 1800s. Among them was the story of Hansel and Gretel, children left to starve in the forest, who came upon a house made of bread and sugar decorations. The hungry children feasted on its sweet shingles. After the fairy tale was published, German bakers began baking houses of lebkuchen—that soft gingerbread—and employed artists and craftsmen to decorate them. The houses were particularly popular during Christmas, a tradition that crossed the ocean with German immigrants. Pennsylvania, where many settled, remains a stronghold for the gingerbread house tradition.

Gingerbread Men

I'M NOT A FAN OF BEAUTIFUL-LOOKING but hard-as-a-rock gingerbread cookies, so I've adapted this recipe with the goal of giving you a wonderful eating experience. These gingerbread men are deep, dark, molasses-rich, and moist. They will keep for ages, but perhaps it's best to not let them sit too long, because you might start to feel like they're family—and it's not in good form to bite a relative's head off.

Makes 3 to 4 dozen 2½-inch-tall gingerbread men cookies

1. Preheat the oven to 350 degrees F. Line 2 cookies sheets with parchment paper and set aside.

2. Sift together the flour, baking soda, salt, ginger, cloves, and cinnamon in a large bowl. Set aside.

3. In the bowl of an electric mixer fitted with the paddle attachment, cream the butter, sugar, and molasses until thoroughly combined on medium-high speed, about 5 minutes. Stir in water and mix until incorporated. The dough will be wet and "broken" (strangely lumpy), but this goes away when you add the flour.

4. Add the flour mixture to the wet ingredients in 3 to 4 additions, mixing on low speed just until incorporated, scraping the sides of the bowl with a rubber spatula as needed. The mixture will be extremely thick. Form the dough into 2 flattened disks and wrap in plastic wrap; let chill for at least 2 hours.

5. Lightly flour your countertop or a large board. Roll the dough ¼ inch thick, using a metal spatula to help lift and turn the dough occasionally, and dust with extra flour as needed to keep it from sticking. Using a gingerbread man cookie cutter, cut the cookies. If desired, make slight variations by hand (using a toothpick or skewer) to personalize the cookies. Arrange them on the prepared baking sheets. Chill for 30 minutes in the refrigerator to help them hold their shapes while baking.

6. Bake for 10 to 12 minutes, or until no imprint remains when the cookies are touched lightly.

5½ cups all-purpose flour

1 teaspoon baking soda

1 teaspoon salt

1 teaspoon ground ginger

1 teaspoon ground cloves

1 teaspoon ground cinnamon

5 tablespoons unsalted butter, softened

1 cup packed dark brown sugar

1½ cups dark molasses

⅔ cup cold water

Writing icing, candies, or sprinkles, for garnish (optional)

7. Remove the cookies from the oven and let them cool on the sheets for 5 minutes. Using a metal spatula, transfer the cookies to wire racks to cool completely.

8. Personalize your cookies further, if desired, by decorating with writing icing, candies, and/or sprinkles.

9. Store at room temperature in an airtight container for up to 10 days (in a single layer, if you've applied icing), or store in the freezer for up to 2 months.

Opera Cake

THE OPERA CAKE, LIKE ITS NAMESAKE, is a work in several acts: an intense, intricate work of artistry that, when it comes together, is an oeuvre in the mouth. It's an elaborate confection, composed of layers of thin almond cake, each soaked in coffee syrup, stacked with coffee cream filling, bittersweet chocolate ganache, and then finished with chocolate glaze, and it's a beauty to behold. Served in squares or rectangles that accentuate its clean lines and precise craftsmanship, a very authentic opera cake boasts its signature written across the top, with a little gold leaf for a dramatic finish.

. . . .

While in America we call it opera cake, in its native France it's known as either *l'opéra* or *gâteau opéra*. Now, I don't know about you, but this dessert is definitely fancier than many of the cakes I bake or eat, which begs the question: is there a difference between gâteau and cake? Sort of. *Gâteau* is a French term that refers, fairly indiscriminately, to any number of different cakes; today, perhaps owing to sweets such as the opera cake, it's a term more generally used for a multilayered cake extravaganza. For instance, you wouldn't call a simple layer cake with candles a birthday gâteau, but you might if it was split into four levels, filled with fancy-flavored buttercreams, wrapped in fondant, or topped with ganache. So a gâteau is a cake, but a cake is not necessarily a gâteau. The idea that I always informally carry in my mind is that the true difference between a gâteau and a cake is the price tag.

L'Opéra is said to have made its grand debut in the early 1900s in Paris, at the Exposition Culinaire. But that wasn't its name, not yet. It was introduced as *gâteau Clichy*, named after its originator,

> *Gâteau is a French term that refers, fairly indiscriminately, to any number of different cakes; today, perhaps owing to sweets such as the opera cake, it's a term more generally used for a multilayered cake extravaganza.*

the gourmet grocer Louis Clichy. "Clichy" was emblazoned on top of it when it was served at the exposition.

So yes, Clichy must be given some credit for developing this cake. But today, not many would refer to the cake by that name. Because it was another bakery that made the cake an international superstar: Dalloyau. Dalloyau, which is pronounced something like "Dal-oh-yoww" (but in your Frenchiest voice), is a Parisian pâtisserie with a serious pedigree (it's said that this fancy bakery has owners who served Louis XIV). They reintroduced a version of the cake as L'Opéra, coinciding with a huge showing by the Paris Grand Opera. It was an instant hit, and has proliferated on bakery menus in France and beyond ever since.

Dalloyau is still known, years later, as the finest purveyor of the stuff. Famed writer on Parisian pastry arts, Dorie Greenspan, says it's still the best, citing that the pastry chef makes "a cake as sleek and smooth as an opera stage and as gloriously delicious as *La Bohème* is affectingly beautiful." This recipe is inspired by their famous version, but streamlined: it uses ganache for the sides and top of the cake, rather than a different recipe for the top.

Opera Cake

THIS CAKE IS PROOF THAT PASTRIES ARE THE ULTIMATE affordable luxury: while not everyone can afford opera tickets, this cake, assembled in "acts," is akin to an operatic experience—an indulgence that's pricey but not unattainable. Making this regal cake is definitely a labor of love, and it requires quite a bit of time and energy, but your resulting dessert will be a splendid affair that will make guests want to eat with pinkies fully extended.

Makes one 10-by-8-inch cake (8 servings)

1. Preheat the oven to 350 degrees F. Line the bottom of 2 (approximately 10-by-15-inch) jelly roll pans with parchment paper. Spray the paper with nonstick spray for easy removal later.

2. In the very clean, dry bowl of a stand mixer fitted with the whisk attachment, beat the egg whites and granulates sugar until stiff peaks form. Transfer to another bowl.

3. In a separate bowl, use a large hand-held whisk to beat the egg yolks until well combined. Add the ground almonds, confectioners' sugar, and pastry flour, mixing only until incorporated. Stir in the melted butter, then fold in the beaten egg whites. Spread the batter evenly into the prepared pans, smoothing and leveling the tops with an offset metal spatula (an offset metal spatula works great for these large cakes).

4. Bake for 10 to 15 minutes, or until the centers spring back when lightly touched and the edges of the cakes have pulled away slightly from the sides. Invert the cakes onto a heatproof flat surface lined with clean parchment paper and peel off the parchment paper used for paper. Let cool completely before proceeding. Make the other components of the cake now, then proceed with assembly.

5. To assemble the cake, cut each sheet of cake in half crosswise so you have 4 roughly 5-by-8-inch rectangles. You will use only 3 of these pieces, so if you make a mistake you'll have a back-up cake; or, you could also feel free to add an extra layer, or use the cake for another dessert.

6. Place one cake layer on a sheet of parchment paper over a sheet of cardboard slightly larger than the cake as a work space. Brush it with

3 egg whites

6 egg yolks

½ cup granulated sugar

1½ cups finely ground almonds

1½ cups confectioners' sugar

½ cup pastry flour

3 tablespoons unsalted butter, melted

½ cup Coffee Syrup (recipe follows)

1½ cups Chocolate Ganache (recipe follows)

3 cups Coffee Cream Filling (recipe follows)

half of the coffee syrup. Spread with half of the chocolate ganache to make an even layer about as thick as the cake layer. Top with another layer of cake, soak it with the remaining coffee syrup, and then spread an even layer of the coffee buttercream frosting, also about as thick as the cake, over that. Top with the third cake layer. Cover in plastic wrap, and chill in the refrigerator 1 hour.

7. To finish, heat the remaining ganache in a double boiler over simmering water until liquid. Place the cake on a rack over parchment paper (to catch drips) and pour the warm ganache over the top, completely covering the surface, using an offset spatula to spread if necessary. Chill the cake in the refrigerator until the ganache is firm.

8. To serve, using a long sharp knife (and cleaning it between slices) trim about ½ inch from the sides of the finished cake. Garnish the cake with and cut into 8 pieces.

COFFEE SYRUP

Makes about ½ cup syrup

1. Combine the sugar, water, and coffee in a small saucepan. Bring to a boil, then reduce the heat and simmer 1 minute more. Stir in the coffee until completely incorporated, then set aside.

1 cup sugar

½ cup water

2 tablespoons very strong brewed coffee

CHOCOLATE GANACHE

Makes about 1½ cups ganache

1. In a medium saucepan over medium heat, bring the cream to a boil. Once boiling, pour it over the chopped chocolate in a large bowl. Stir slowly until it has melted together and the mixture is smooth. Let cool to room temperature before spreading.

2 cups heavy cream

14 ounces semisweet chocolate, finely chopped (about 2 cups)

1 cup sugar

¼ cup water

3 egg whites

1¼ cups (2½ sticks) unsalted butter, cut into pieces, at room temperature

1 tablespoon very strong brewed coffee, such as espresso

COFFEE CREAM FILLING

 Makes 3 cups filling

1. In a small saucepan over medium-high heat, combine the sugar and water. Stir until the sugar is dissolved, brushing down the sides of the pan so that no sugar crystals remain, then stop stirring and continue heating the mixture until it boils. Heat to 240 degrees F on a candy thermometer (soft-ball stage). Remove the syrup from the burner when it reaches the correct temperature.

2. Concurrently, when the syrup reaches 230 degrees F, begin beating the egg whites with an electric mixer on medium speed. They should attain soft peaks.

3. When the syrup is ready, with the mixer on low speed, pour the syrup into the egg whites in a gradual, steady stream, being careful not to splash the hot liquid. Increase the speed to high; once the whites have attained full height, turn the mixer to medium speed and continue to beat until the mixture is at room temperature. (Feel the side of the bowl to make sure you do not feel any heat.) Beat in the butter, a little at a time, and the coffee, until the frosting is smooth. Wait until it is room temperature before spreading. If not using immediately, refrigerate, then whisk before using.

Princess Torte

THERE ARE CERTAIN UNEXPLAINED MYSTERIES OF THE UNIVERSE:
What is the meaning of life? If a tree falls in the forest, can anybody hear it?
Why do we continue to watch reality TV? But here's a sweet mystery that is
far more pleasurable to explore: What is the princess torte, and why is it green?

. . . .

When we're talking princess torte, we are not talking about princess cake,
that fixture at six-year-old girls' birthday parties, composed of a severed Barbie
doll perched atop a dome of cake covered with frilly buttercream to resemble
a dress. No, the cake we're talking about hails from Sweden, where it's referred
to as *Princesstårta*. This pinkies-out confection—a pretty dome-shaped cake
that's made of alternating layers of light, airy cake; thick pastry cream; and
jam, all topped with a sweet jacket of tinted marzipan—is not as common in
bakery cases as say, red velvet cake, but it's not an exceedingly rare cake either.
Most urban areas will have at least a couple of bakeries that offer a version.
But perhaps the most striking thing about this cake is how the outer layer of
marzipan is *nearly always green*. Oh, you will see it other ways—you may see
it with pink or cream marzipan, or even with chocolate—but most likely it
will be green. And a very distinct type of green—sort of an Easter pastel, baby
pistachio green.

The reason for the unusual color of the cake has stumped pastry chefs for
a long time: Perhaps it was the princess's favorite color? Perhaps it was col-
ored to reflect the princess's wedding flowers? Or perhaps green was a color
that caught on with the Swedish audience because it represented the hope of
spring, like the first gentle blades of grass coming up after a cold, dark winter?

But we can make some educated guesses based on the cake's past. It had its
beginnings in the influential *Prinsessornas Kokbok*, or "Princesses Cookbook,"

The reason for the unusual color of the cake has stumped pastry chefs for a long time: Perhaps it was the princess's favorite color?

published in the 1930s by Jenny Åkerström, the owner of a popular Swedish cooking school. The book, while named for the princesses of the royal family at the time (Margaret, Märtha, and Astrid), is really quite a comprehensive guide to traditional Swedish cuisine. In the dessert chapter, there are a number of elaborate tortes, including three named after each of the princesses. And while today's princess torte has similarities to each of these cakes, it's not a definite derivation of any of them. The most striking in physical resemblance is Princess Martha's special torte: it's covered with green-tinted marzipan leaves, and topped with a pink flower. In a later holiday spinoff of the book, the dessert offerings evolved to include *Grön tårta*, or "green cake"; it's just called princess torte because the princesses were said to have been especially fond of the cake.

Today's princess torte has evolved a lot since those girls were playing in the royal courtyard. It's a reflection of the original cakes designed for the princesses, with further liberties taken: a layer of jam added here, nuts removed there. But the green dome, possibly an easier version of that leaf pattern mentioned in the original recipe for Martha's cake, has stayed in the picture.

Princess Torte

THE PRINCESS TORTE IS TRULY ONE FIT FOR ROYALTY. For ease, consider making this recipe over several days: the cake and custard will both hold for up to three days, wrapped well and stored in your fridge. This recipe is adapted from a recipe in Grey Patent's *A Baker's Odyssey*, which I discovered via Helene Dujardin of TarteletteBlog.com.

Makes one 9-inch layer cake (10 to 12 servings)

1. Using a serrated knife, cut the cake horizontally into 3 equal layers. Set aside for the moment.

2. In a stand mixer fitted with the whisk attachment, whip the heavy cream until thick and firm, but not grainy. Transfer one-third of the cream to a small bowl, cover, and refrigerate.

3. Remove the chilled custard from the refrigerator and give it a vigorous whisk, as it may have thickened. Make sure it is smooth and creamy before proceeding. Fold the whipped cream that you did not refrigerate into the custard and stir gently until smooth.

4. Set the bottom cake layer, cut side up, on a serving platter. To keep the plate clean as you frost and decorate the cake, you can place parchment paper in strips around the bottom edges of the cake, tucked gently under it—or just clean off the plate before serving.

5. Spread the raspberry jam onto the top of the cake layer, leaving a ¼-inch margin all around. On top of this, spread half of the cream filling. Invert the middle cake layer onto the custard cream, cut side up. Spread the remaining cream filling over this second layer; top with the final layer of cake. Spread about one-quarter of the refrigerated whipped cream in a very thin layer around the sides of the torte. With an offset spatula, evenly spread the remaining whipped cream onto the top of the torte. Remove the paper strips from underneath the torte and refrigerate the torte for about 1 hour. This will help the torte "set" and keep it firm while you add your marzipan topping.

6. Lightly dust a space for rolling with sifted confectioners' sugar. Place the marzipan on the powdered sugar and dust the top of the

One 9-inch Sponge Cake (recipe follows)

2½ cups heavy cream

2¼ cups Custard Filling (recipe follows)

⅓ cup seedless raspberry jam

Confectioners' sugar, for rolling the marzipan

Marzipan Dome (recipe follows)

A pink flower and pink ribbon, for decoration (optional)

marzipan. Roll out the marzipan to ¼ inch thick. Using a brush, dust off any extra confectioners' sugar.

7. Remove the torte from the refrigerator and gently set the marzipan on top so that it drapes over the torte. Press it gently so it adheres to the sides of the torte, covering it completely. With a sharp knife, trim away any excess marzipan so that the edges are clean.

8. If desired, run a length of pink ribbon around the bottom edge of the torte. Not only does this look pretty, but it covers up any hacking you might have done to the bottom edges of the cake! Place the pink flower on the top of the torte (you could use frosting to make a buttercream flower, too). Refrigerate until ready to serve. When serving, it is helpful to run a sharp knife under hot water and then dry the blade before cutting; this will ensure clean cuts.

9. Store, well wrapped, in the refrigerator for up to 3 days.

SPONGE CAKE

Makes one 9-inch cake

- ¾ cup all-purpose flour
- ¼ cup potato starch (found in specialty supermarkets)
- ½ teaspoon baking powder
- 4 large eggs, separated
- ⅛ teaspoon salt
- ¾ cup plus 2 tablespoons granulated sugar

1. Preheat the oven to 350 degrees F. Grease and flour the bottom and sides of a 9-by-4-inch springform pan; line the bottom of the pan with a circle of parchment paper.

2. Sift together the flour, potato starch, and baking powder in a small bowl. Set aside.

3. In a stand mixer with a very clean bowl and fitted with the whisk attachment, whip the egg whites and salt on medium speed until the whites form stiff, shiny peaks. Transfer to a separate bowl.

4. Wash the bowl and whisk attachment for your electric mixer; use again to beat the egg yolks. Combine the egg yolks and sugar, beating on medium speed until ribbons have formed. Add the egg whites back to the mixing bowl, and beat on low speed until incorporated. Remove the bowl from the mixer.

5. Gently fold in the flour mixture in 3 additions, making sure it is fully incorporated. Pour the batter into the prepared pan.

6. Bake for about 30 minutes, or until the cake is golden brown and a toothpick inserted into the center comes out clean. Cool the cake in the pan on a wire rack for 10 minutes. Run a knife around the side of the cake, release the cake from the pan, and invert onto a wire rack. Let it cool completely before assembling the torte.

CUSTARD FILLING

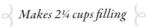

Makes 2¼ cups filling

½ vanilla bean, scraped with pod
Pinch salt
2 cups whole milk
2 tablespoons cornstarch
2 large eggs
½ cup sugar

1. To make the custard, combine the vanilla bean, seeds, salt, and 1½ cups of the milk in a medium saucepan. Bring to a boil.

2. In a medium bowl, whisk together the cornstarch and sugar. Add the remaining ½ cup milk and whisk until smooth. Add the eggs to the cornstarch mixture and whisk to combine.

3. When the milk comes to a boil, whisk part of it into the egg mixture and then transfer everything to the saucepan, again while whisking. Continue whisking vigorously while the custard thickens and boils for 1 minute. Transfer to another bowl, cover the top of the custard directly with plastic wrap or parchment, and allow to cool completely in the refrigerator.

MARZIPAN DOME

Makes 1½ pounds marzipan

1½ pounds marzipan (found in specialty supermarkets)
Several drops green food coloring
Confectioners' sugar, for rolling

1. To make the marzipan dome, color a walnut-sized piece of marzipan with the green food coloring until the piece is deep green. Reserve.

2. Using a sifter, dust a work surface with confectioners' sugar. Knead a small piece of the green marzipan into the remaining uncolored marzipan until it is uniform in color. Add additional pieces from the green marzipan until it achieves a light green color. Discard the left-over deep green marzipan.

3. Keep the marzipan at room temperature if it is to be used within 24 hours. Otherwise, store the marzipan double-wrapped in plastic in the refrigerator.

COMMERCIAL FAVORITES

THEY'RE A SPECIAL PART OF OUR LIVES: those sweet nothings, those prepackaged lunchbox icons that remain beloved into adulthood. Many of these store-bought creations have fascinating stories of invention, ranging from scandalous to sometimes, well, just plain strange. Here's a celebration of these commercially produced treats, including some home recipes inspired by these classics.

Animal Crackers

"Animal crackers and cocoa to drink
that is the finest of suppers I think;
when I am grown up and have what I please
I think I shall always insist upon these."

—ACTOR AND WRITER CHRISTOPHER MORLEY,
SONGS FOR A LITTLE HOUSE

EVERYONE LOVES THOSE CURIOUS ANIMAL-SHAPED cookies that pack a crunch and are called "crackers." But how is it that these proud little animals began marching their way into our mouths and hearts?

. . . .

Well. The custom of crafting cookies that resemble creatures is nothing new—as early as the 1600s in Germany, bakers were making sweet treats resembling savage beasts. But it wasn't until the 1800s that the wheels began to turn, setting off the chain reaction that made these sweet crackers a snacking staple. For this we owe a thank-you to the industrial revolution: that's when biscuits, cookies, and crackers began to be manufactured in factories. In Victorian England, "crisp biscuits"—that's sweet, cracker-like cookies, to Americans—were very popular. Some of these biscuits were shaped like animals.

A hint of things to come was evident when Zoologicals, animal-shaped cookies made by Philadelphia baker Walter G. Wilson, were sold at the Centennial Exposition of 1876—the first world's fair in America. (This pivotal event yielded many innovations, including the introduction of the Dewey Decimal system, the ice cream soda, and the grand debut of the Statue of Liberty's torch, before it was affixed to the rest of her body in New York City.)

After acquiring two New York City bakeries that produced animal-shaped biscuits, the National Biscuit Company (later Nabisco) began producing animal-shaped biscuits on a commercial scale which allowed for widespread

The custom of crafting cookies that resemble creatures is nothing new—as early as the 1600s in Germany, bakers were making sweet treats resembling savage beasts.

distribution. Serendipitously, this timing coincided with P. T. Barnum's growing reputation as an international showman and circus owner. Perhaps sensing a sales opportunity, several companies had begun marketing foods of all sorts with circus-themed packaging, and these biscuits were a natural tie-in. The National Biscuit Company did it most famously, with their 1902 debut of the animal-shaped crackers. Marketed as a specialty holiday item, they were sold in a small box resembling a circus cage with a handle at the top, for displaying as an ornament.

The crackers proved so popular that they were soon being produced year-round, the ornament string promoted as an easy way for children to transport the cookies. In 1948, they were renamed Barnum's Animal Crackers, which is what they're still called today. But for all the glittering success of the Barnum association, the circus man did not receive payment for the use of his name: according to an article in the *Washington Post*, he never got a cent for the crackers.

Animal Crackers

ATTAINING THE DRY, CRACKER-LIKE TEXTURE of commercially produced animal crackers is tough to achieve in a standard home oven. While slightly softer than the original, these biscuits are nonetheless nostalgically delicious.

Makes 6 dozen small cookies

1. In a medium bowl, stir together the flour, baking powder, salt, and cinnamon. Set aside.

2. In the bowl of a stand mixer fitted with the paddle attachment, cream the butter and sugar on medium speed until light and fluffy, 3 to 5 minutes. Add the egg and vanilla, stirring until combined.

3. Add the flour mixture in 3 additions, mixing after each addition just until incorporated. Scrape down the sides of the bowl as needed.

4. Form the dough into 2 disks and wrap well with plastic; refrigerate for at least 2 hours or overnight. Chilling the dough will ensure that the shapes hold once cut out and that the dough will not spread too much during baking.

5. Preheat the oven to 350 degrees F. Line 2 baking sheets with parchment paper and set aside.

6. Allow the cookie dough to warm slightly at room temperature before rolling it. On a floured work surface, use a floured rolling pin to roll the dough to about ¼ inch thick. Use small animal-shaped cutters to cut the dough (of course, other small cutters will work, too). Using a metal spatula, transfer the cookies to the prepared baking sheets. Gather up the dough scraps and re-roll to make more cookies. Leave a small amount of room around each cookie to allow for spreading. If desired, you can use toothpicks to enhance the details on the animals, or add faces.

7. Let the cookies chill (on the baking sheets) in the refrigerator for 30 minutes before baking. This will ensure even further that the dough retains any details you've added.

2½ cups all-purpose flour

¼ teaspoon salt

1 teaspoon baking powder

⅛ teaspoon cinnamon

¾ cup (1½ sticks) unsalted butter, softened to cool room temperature

1 cup sugar

1 egg

1½ teaspoons vanilla extract

8. Bake for 12 to 15 minutes, or until firm, just lightly brown on the edges, and with a dull finish on top. Let cool on the pan for several minutes, then transfer to a flat surface (they may fall through a wire rack) to cool completely. Store the cookies in an airtight container for up to 7 days.

FASCINATING FACTS ABOUT BARNUM'S ANIMAL CRACKERS

* The designer of the famous circus-themed packaging, Sydney Stern, was an artist hired by Nabisco in 1923; he spent his career designing several of the snack company's most famous packages, including Animal Crackers (which have only changed slightly over the years!), Ritz Crackers, and Shredded Wheat.

* Each machine-filled box is filled at random with 22 biscuits, so you never know what critters your menagerie will contain.

* Per Panati's *Extraordinary Origins of Everyday Things*, children across America tend to "nibble away at the animals in definite order of dismemberment: back legs, forelegs, head, and lastly the body."

* It's generally accepted that the Animal Crackers' success is what spurred Nabisco to develop a bevy of other biscuits, including the Oreo.

* In the 1900s, the cost for a box was 4 cents. Today, they cost around $1.49.

Girl Scout Cookies

AH, GIRL SCOUT COOKIE SEASON: that special time of the year when young girls congregate near store entrances and tempt the hungry and tired with their sweet wares. Somehow, I never seem to be able to escape their earnest sales pitch without committing to buying a dozen boxes. After all, it *is* for a good cause, and the cookies are nothing short of addictive. But you know, it wasn't always a business enterprise. Here's how it went from at-home activity to nationwide phenomenon.

. . . .

In the beginning, cookie baking was a simple activity that Girl Scouts did at home with their mothers. That didn't last for long, however: within five years after the Girl Scouts of America got its start, selling cookies—the homemade kind—was used as a fundraising method, with very successful results. The tradition only continued to grow, and with it their status as miniature Gordon Gekkos in green plaid skirts.

In 1932, the first formal sale took place in Philadelphia, where the girls baked their cookies and sold them from the city's gas and electric company windows; a commemorative plaque marks the building today. The response was so good that they realized their time was better spent selling, not baking: next thing you knew, the cookies were being commercially produced by approved bakeries in the shape of the Girl Scout trefoil. Enthusiasm for the cookies spread nationwide, and in 1937, more than 125 Girl Scout councils reported holding cookie sales.

Since then, the cookies have pretty much been sold annually, save a few limited-production years during World War II, when sugar, flour, and butter shortages led Girl Scouts to sell calendars to raise money for their activities instead. After the war, cookies were back and better than ever.

The cookies have pretty much been sold annually, save a few limited-production years during World War II, when sugar, flour, and butter shortages led Girl Scouts to sell calendars to raise money for their activities instead.

By that time, the cookies came in several flavors, including Shortbread and Chocolate Mints (the precursor to today's Thin Mints). In a way, it was this expansion that eventually led to the assortment of cookies that we know today. Currently, two licensed bakers produce a maximum of eight varieties, including three mandatory ones (Thin Mints, Peanut Butter Sandwiches, and Shortbread Trefoils).

The Girl Scout cookie tradition hasn't been without a few bumps in the road. There have been a few price wars between neighboring towns, and recently, due to the rising costs of ingredients and transportation, the number of cookies in each box has gone down. (To date, nobody has cited the *positive* effect of these reduced portions on our collective waistlines.) But really, we ought not perceive these actions negatively; after all, the profits do go toward supporting the venerable Girl Scouts of America.

Scout Butter Cookies

TODAY, WHILE THIN MINTS ARE the undisputed bestseller, there's something to be said about the simplicity of the earliest versions of these cookies, which evolved into today's Shortbread Trefoils. What follows is an adaptation of that early recipe from the Girl Scout magazine; while the cookie was originally rolled as a cutout cookie, I've updated it a bit as a slice-and-bake cookie for easier home baking.

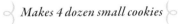 *Makes 4 dozen small cookies*

1. In a medium bowl, sift together the flour, baking powder, and salt.

2. In the bowl of a stand mixer fitted with the paddle attachment, cream the butter and sugar on high speed until light and fluffy, 2 to 3 minutes.

3. Add the eggs, one at a time, pausing to scrape down the sides of the bowl with a rubber spatula after each addition. Mix in the milk and vanilla, then add the flour mixture in 2 to 3 additions, mixing just until incorporated, again scraping the bowl as needed.

4. Divide the dough into 2 equal portions. Roll the dough into several logs (3 or 4), each about 1 foot long and a little over 1 inch in diameter. Wrap them tightly in plastic wrap. Refrigerate until thoroughly chilled, at least 2 hours or overnight.

5. Preheat the oven to 375 degrees F. Line 2 baking sheets with parchment paper. You may have to bake in batches and reuse one of the pans.

6. Remove the dough from the refrigerator (one log at a time). Slice into coins of dough, about ¼ inch thick. Transfer the cookies to the prepared sheets, leaving about 1½ inches on all sides to allow for spreading. Bake for 8 to 10 minutes, or until the edges just begin to brown. Allow the cookies to cool on the sheets for 5 minutes before transferring to a wire rack to cool completely.

7. Store in an airtight container at room temperature for up to 4 days, or store in the freezer for up to 1 month.

2 cups all-purpose flour

2 teaspoons baking powder

½ teaspoon salt

1 cup (2 sticks) unsalted butter

1 cup sugar

2 large eggs

2 tablespoons whole or 2% milk

½ teaspoon vanilla extract

WHAT'S IN A NAME? SWEET STORIES BEHIND SNACK CAKES WITH CURIOUS NAMES.

DEVIL DOGS: A combination of cake type and construction led to this unusual name: unfrosted devil's food cake sandwiches are gently folded around the filling on one side, which makes them (sort of) resemble hot dogs.

DING DONGS: These chocolate-covered, hockey puck–shaped, cream-filled cakes were named to coincide with a TV ad campaign featuring a ringing bell. Don't mistake them for Ring Dings, a similar snack made by Drake's Cakes that was purchased by Hostess and absorbed into the greater Ding Dong world.

HO HOS: Resembling mini roulade cakes, made from chocolate cake rolled with vanilla cream filling and coated with a thin layer of chocolate, these treats were named for a jovial mascot with a hearty laugh, named Happy Ho Ho.

KRIMPETS: Originally, these snack cakes would crumble in eager hands, so the manufacturer "crimped" the pan to make the cakes easier to hold; perhaps the K was a style choice in keeping with their company name, TastyKakes.

SNO BALLS: These balls of marshmallow-and-coconut-coated cake happiness were originally all white, but to add a little pizzazz in the 1950s, Hostess started tinting the cakes and including one white and one pink in each pack. This proved too strenuous, apparently, and ultimately the pink survived. The white ones are available seasonally, during winter months.

SUZY Q'S: Sweet, sweet nepotism. These unfrosted, oblong banana or chocolate cream–filled sandwich cakes, developed in 1961, are named for the daughter of the Continental Baking Company's vice president.

TWINKIES: On a meeting to pitch the quintessential all-American snack cake, inventor James Dewar got his idea for the name when driving by a billboard advertising Twinkle Toe Shoes, which he shortened to Twinkies.

ZINGERS: These snack cakes have a little "zing" that comes from their frosting—or, in the case of the raspberry zinger, their raspberry and coconut coating.

Chocolate Creme-Filled Cookies

HOLD ON TO YOUR HATS, OREO LOVERS, because I've got a secret to tell you: America's favorite sandwich cookies, those twin chocolate wafer rounds filled with the addictive "creme" filling, were actually preceded by another—the Hydrox cookie. This may come as a surprise, especially given the fact that the Hydrox has always seemed to play second fiddle to the more famous cookie that ultimately eclipsed them. But it's time to face the truth.

. . . .

The chocolate wafer cookies filled with vanilla icing known as Hydrox made their debut in 1908, a product of the Sunshine Biscuit label. Its name was taken from the atomic elements that make up pure water: hydrogen and oxygen. Maybe this was done to put out an image of purity—but ultimately, the name comes off sounding somewhat like a cleaning product! In spite of the unfortunate name, however, the cookies proved popular. Or at least popular enough to gain the interest of Nabisco, a rival company.

In 1912, Nabisco debuted a cookie called the Oreo. Like Hydrox cookies, Oreos were a creme-filled chocolate wafer sandwich cookie with a strange name. The fact that Nabisco had released a rival cookie wasn't all that surprising—the two companies had sparred for years with competing products.

In the case of Oreo vs. Hydrox, there really wasn't a whole lot of difference between the cookies. Visually, the imprint designs on each differed, but not a whole lot. Fans of the Hydrox will say it had a "tangy, less sweet filling" and was a crunchier cookie that stood up better in milk. Oreo fans will say that the twist, lick, dunk ritual works better with the Nabisco biscuits.

Oreo even has a street named after it—Oreo Way—in New York City, where the first Oreo cookie was made at the original Nabisco factory.

Perhaps it was a simple case of better marketing (and a better name) that propelled Oreos to the top, but either way, as time went on, more and more people thought that Hydrox cookies were a ripped-off version of the Oreo cookie (I myself can remember turning up my nose to Hydrox cookies as a child— foolish girl). In 1996, Hydrox cookies went through an image change and were released as Droxies, but after the so-called "hipper" version received a lukewarm reception, the Hydrox was ultimately discontinued. On the cookie's one hundredth anniversary, Kellogg's resumed distribution of Hydrox. The cookies were only available nationally for a short time, and now poor, abandoned Hydrox doesn't even appear on the Kellogg's website.

So Oreo might not have been first to the plate, but they won the game. Today, more than a hundred years after its invention, it's the bestselling commercial cookie in America. Oreo even has a street named after it—Oreo Way—in New York City, where the first Oreo cookie was made at the original Nabisco factory. While vestiges of the Hydrox still exist—crumbled Hydrox cookie bits are still sold as "mix-ins" for yogurt or ice cream, and there are websites dedicated to its memory—it is a cookie that exists just there: in our memories.

Chocolate Creme-Filled Cookies

MAKING HOMEMADE SANDWICH COOKIES is a rewarding practice; you'll have fun seeing all those perfectly round little wafers on your countertop, just waiting to be married up with their mate. (Tip: For the perfect twist, adhere the tops only lightly.) Some folks may turn up their noses at the vegetable shortening called for in the filling. While butter will work and taste great, to duplicate the unique, slightly fluffy texture of store-bought varieties, you've gotta use the shortening.

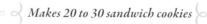

Makes 20 to 30 sandwich cookies

1. In a medium bowl, sift together the flour, cocoa powder, baking soda, baking powder, and salt. Set aside.

2. In the bowl of a stand mixer fitted with the paddle attachment, cream the butter and sugar on medium-high speed until fluffy, 2 to 3 minutes. Beat in the egg until fully incorporated. Stir in the vanilla. Add the flour mixture in 2 to 3 additions, mixing until just incorporated and pausing to scrape the sides of the bowl with a rubber spatula after each addition.

3. Form the dough into 2 flat disks and wrap tightly in plastic wrap; refrigerate until thoroughly chilled, at least 1 hour or overnight.

4. Preheat the oven to 375 degrees F. Line 3 baking sheets with parchment paper (or reuse pans).

5. Generously flour a work surface. Working with 1 disk at a time, roll the cookie dough to about ¼ inch thick, and cut out rounds using an approximately 1½-inch cookie cutter. Gather scraps and re-roll as needed. If the dough becomes too soft, chill to re-firm. Transfer to the baking sheet using a spatula, leaving 1½ inches between cookies to allow for spreading.

6. Bake for 8 to 10 minutes, or until the tops have a dull finish. Let cool on the pans for 5 minutes before transferring to a wire rack to cool completely (they will crisp as they cool).

7. Spread a teaspoon-size dollop of filling on half of the cookies (on the bottom sides); press the remaining cookie halves lightly in place so the cookies adhere to the filling and form sandwiches.

1½ cups all-purpose flour

⅓ cup unsweetened cocoa powder

1 teaspoon baking soda

¼ teaspoon baking powder

½ teaspoon salt

¾ cup unsalted butter, softened but still cool

1 cup sugar

1 large egg

1⅓ cups Creme Filling (recipe follows)

8. Store the cookies in an airtight container for up to 3 days. Note: The filling will soften the crisp cookies; if you prefer crisper cookies, fill immediately before serving.

2 tablespoons unsalted butter, softened

½ cup vegetable shortening

2 cups confectioners' sugar, sifted

Pinch salt

1½ teaspoons vanilla extract

CREME FILLING

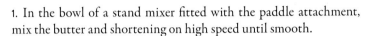 *Makes 1⅓ cups filling*

1. In the bowl of a stand mixer fitted with the paddle attachment, mix the butter and shortening on high speed until smooth.

2. Reduce the speed to low, and beat in the confectioners' sugar, salt, and vanilla. Increase the mixer to high and beat for 3 to 5 minutes, or until the filling is very fluffy.

Pink Frosted Cookies

THERE IS A HAPPY COOKIE WITH A BUTTERY BASE that hovers somewhere between chewy and crunchy, that's capped with a bright pink swirl of frosting, and that proliferates in the northwest United States—especially in the Seattle area. Even though it's widely available, it flies oddly under the radar: while it does hang out in some bakeries, it's more comfortable in places like convenience stores, delis, grocery stores, and even drugstores. It seems like it could be a packaged good available everywhere, along the lines of a Twinkie or Yodel. Let's discuss the interesting series of events that brought it to the Northwest.

....

The original pink frosted cookie is sold under the name Uncle Seth's Cookie. For many years this was an independent company, but it was sold to a larger wholesaler in the area. Pinks Original Bakery, the current owner of the cookie, describes:

"From the high mountain tops of Bali came the inspiration for the feel good cookie. Danny Brown, the originator and inventor of the Original Pink, also known as an Uncle Seth Cookie, found a kindred spirit in a man named Seth. Seth moved from a crazed urban setting better known as the City, to live his dream of peace in the mountains. The namesake of the Uncle Seth Cookie gave tribute to this man named Seth who changed his life for the sake of fun and happiness. To bring a bit of that passion and fun to light, Danny created a cookie that says eat me because you can. This cookie has a good aura. After nine years of hand rolling this Danish Shortbread, Danny too, decided to head for the hills. Mostly Muffins purchased Uncle Seth's Cookies in 1996 and Danny was off to live in Hawaii!"

Turns out, Mr. Pink Cookie had been baking these treats since before his Bali awakening. Danny Brown, who was raised Mormon, had done his mission work in Denmark: it was there that he'd learned how to make Danish

A happy cookie with a buttery base that hovers somewhere between chewy and crunchy, that's capped with a bright pink swirl of frosting.

butter cookies, and would later jokingly refer to his time there as "Pink Cookie Bootcamp." It wasn't until Brown had his serendipitous spiritual meeting in Bali, however, that he decided how to put his cookie-baking prowess to work.

While the cookies still have a stronghold in Utah, they're arguably not as ubiquitous as in the Northwest, where they seem to have hit just the right audience at the right time. Early on, the cookies were mostly sold in coffee carts—and this was just as the coffee business was starting up in earnest in Seattle. Naturally, the pink cookies tempted customers for the same reasons that coffee is so popular in the area—the climate just begs for rich treats and hot drinks during those rainy days that take up, oh, eight months of the year. The second and perhaps more important aspect? Duh—the frosting color. It's no secret that pink frosting tastes better than any other color.

Danny Brown eventually sold his company in Seattle, abandoning the drizzle for sunny Hawaii, where he helped start a bakery. Danny's attention to detail was passed on when he sold the company to Pinks Original Bakery, a wholesaler in Seattle. Even though it's a commercial bakery, they follow the original list of ingredients and mixing instructions—and they still hand-frost each cookie, which also follows a very exacting process, including specific brands of flour, sugar, and flavorings.

Pink Frosted Cookies

THESE ARE A SOFTER, MORE DELICATE VERSION of the pink cookie than Danny's iconic original (the recipe for that is still a secret!). And why not make them a little more luscious, since they don't have to go through the rigors of packaging and traveling to far-off places? These are baked as a drop cookie rather than as a rolled, cut-out cookie—which makes them even friendlier for home bakers. It's an easy recipe, and an opportunity to get a taste of a cookie with a strange but sweet past.

 *Makes 2 dozen cookies*

1. Preheat the oven to 350 degrees F. Line 2 baking sheets with parchment paper and set aside.

2. Sift together the flour, baking powder, and salt; set aside.

3. In the bowl of a stand mixer fitted with the paddle attachment, cream the butter and sugar together on medium speed until light and fluffy, 3 to 5 minutes. Add the eggs one at a time, pausing to scrape down the sides of the bowl with a rubber spatula after each addition. Mix in the milk and vanilla.

4. Reduce the speed to low. Add the flour mixture in 2 to 3 additions, scraping down the bowl as needed, until everything is well blended. Drop the cookie dough by heaping spoonfuls onto the prepared baking sheets, leaving 1½ to 2 inches around each cookie to allow for spreading.

5. Bake for 10 to 12 minutes, or until the tops of the cookies spring back to the touch, like the top of a cake (they will remain fairly light in color). Leave the cookies on the tray for several minutes, then use a metal spatula to transfer them to a wire rack to cool completely before frosting.

6. Spread the frosting in a thick layer on top of the cookies.

7. Store in a single layer in an airtight container at cool room temperature for up to 3 days.

5 cups all-purpose flour

1 tablespoon baking powder

½ teaspoon salt

1 cup (2 sticks) unsalted butter, softened

2 cups sugar

4 large eggs

1 cup whole or 2% milk

1 teaspoon vanilla extract

3 cups Pink Frosting (recipe follows)

Sprinkles, for garnish (optional)

1 cup (2 sticks) unsalted butter, softened

1½ teaspoons vanilla extract

6 cups confectioners' sugar

2 tablespoons whole or 2% milk

About 6 drops red food coloring

PINK FROSTING

 Makes 3 cups frosting

1. In a stand mixer fitted with the paddle attachment, beat the butter and vanilla until smooth. On low speed, gradually beat in the sugar 1 cup at a time, until your desired consistency has been reached. If the mixture becomes too thick, thin it with the milk. Stir in the food coloring, drop by drop, until your desired pink hue is achieved Cover the frosting tightly and keep it chilled until you're ready to frost the cupcakes.

Toaster-Style Pastries

POP-TARTS LINE HALF AN AISLE IN THE SUPERMARKET; they've been the star of memorable television commercials; they're ubiquitous in office vending machines. Even if you don't eat them on a regular basis, these slim-profiled pockets of filled pastry, perfectly sized to fit in a typical toaster, have certainly become part of our everyday American landscape.

. . . .

Pop-Tarts were invented in the post–World War II era, when the Post company was developing new products, trying to satisfy a demand for foods that were convenient and had a long shelf life. The now-familiar foil packaging was originally used as a way of preserving a type of moist dog food; Post altered it slightly to accommodate a new people-food treat that they called Country Squares. Unfortunately, loose-lipped employees shared the secret of the product in development before it was released, giving their rival, Kellogg's, a chance to come up with a competitive product—and obviously to think up a better name.

In 1992, when a toaster failed to eject a Pop-Tart and the would-be eater's kitchen caught on fire, the Pop-Tart briefly suffered a reputation as a snack that could kill you.

Kellogg's was able to bring the pastries to market in short order, with a name that worked on a double level, referring to not only the product but to the Pop Art movement of the era. Pop-Tarts took the market by storm, advertised by an animated toaster named Milton; the company literally could not keep shelves stocked. The first Pop-Tarts came out in four flavors: strawberry, blueberry, brown sugar–cinnamon, and apple currant. The first three are still with us. The fate of Country Squares? Well, when's the last time you saw a box at your local grocery store?

When the tarts made their 1964 debut, their role as breakfast superstar was not yet clear. Retailers were actually urged by the manufacturer to place the tarts in the bakery or the cake mix section of their store, rather than in the cereal section. The original Pop-Tarts were also unfrosted, the thought being that the frosting might melt and cause problems in the toaster. Happily, great minds were put to work on the issue, and a toaster-safe frosted version came out in 1967.

The life of the Pop-Tart hasn't been without its share of woes, though. In the early 1990s, there was an unfortunate bout of toaster clogging in the United Kingdom, where it turns out their toasters, like their accents, are different from ours. In 1992, when a toaster failed to eject a Pop-Tart and the would-be eater's kitchen caught on fire, the Pop-Tart briefly suffered a reputation as a snack that could kill you. Kellogg's has made some bad decisions, too: consider the ill-fated addition of Go-Tarts (slender Pop-Tart sticks meant for on-the-go consumption) to the line—which is definitely not as fun as cramming an entire Pop-Tart in your mouth, judging by their speedy discontinuation. There have also been flavor hits (the most excellent S'more Pop-Tart), and misses (I, for one, did not find the neon-toned Wild! Berry tarts appetizing).

But like so many things we create ourselves, half the fun of making these treats is getting to decide on the important individual touches—like what kind of filling you want to use. The possibilities are almost endless, so don't feel you're limited to jams and other fruit-based products. Who says you can't have a tart filled with chocolaty Nutella or your sister's famous rum-spiked caramel? Or how about inventing a savory filling, like an herbed goat cheese mixture?

Toaster-Style Pastries

THESE TARTS ARE A BELOVED PART of our culture—a quick breakfast that tends to be favored by the young but that carries warm memories for us all.

Makes 6 to 8 pastries

FOR THE PASTRY:

1½ cups all-purpose flour

1 teaspoon salt

½ cup (1 stick) butter, chilled and cut into cubes

3 tablespoons cold whole or 2% milk

About ½ cup jam, preserves, peanut butter, ganache, or other filling of your choice

FOR THE ICING:

1 cup confectioners' sugar, sifted

2 tablespoons milk or heavy cream, plus extra as needed

FOR GARNISH:

Sprinkles (optional)

1. Preheat the oven to 450 degrees F. Line a baking sheet with parchment paper and set aside.

2. To make the dough, combine the flour and salt in a large bowl. Add the butter and cut into the flour using 2 forks or a pastry cutter. Blend until the mixture resembles coarse crumbs. Add the milk, bit by bit, gently mixing the dough after each addition, until the dough forms a ball (you may not need all the milk).

3. Place the dough on a lightly floured surface and roll it into a large rectangle, about ⅛ inch thick. Cut out rectangles approximately the size of index cards (3 by 5 inches), or smaller if you prefer a more modest portion. Make sure you have an even number of cutouts.

4. Transfer half of the rectangles to your prepared baking sheet (if they're hard to handle, use a metal spatula to transfer the pieces). On half of the rectangles, place 1 tablespoon of jam or other filling in the center. Add another plain rectangle on top of each piece, pressing down gently to spread the filling toward the edges.

5. Crimp all 4 edges of the pastry with the tines of a fork to ensure that the filling doesn't ooze out. Poke the top of each pastry with the fork to allow steam to vent.

6. Bake for 7 to 9 minutes, or until light golden on the edges. Remove from the oven and let cool completely.

7. To make the icing, in a medium bowl, mix the confectioners' sugar with just enough milk to make a glaze that is thick but still pourable. Drizzle it over the cooled pastries. Garnish with sprinkles immediately.

8. These tarts are best served warm. Since the homemade treats are not necessarily "toaster stable" (I know, I know), reheat in a toaster oven on a low toasting setting for 2 to 3 minutes rather than in a conventional toaster.

CURIOUS
CONFECTIONS

SOME BAKED GOODS ARE A LITTLE DIFFERENT from others. In this chapter, we celebrate these items, ranging from sweets with strange names to unusual urban legends to pies associated with political-religious movements. There's even a bit of sex and drugs thrown in. These unique desserts may first grab your attention with their stories, but they'll reward you with great taste, too.

Alice B. Toklas Brownies

I KNOW, I KNOW. IT READS LIKE AN URBAN LEGEND: pot brownies named after Alice B. Toklas. But believe it or not, the famed salon hostess and longtime Gertrude Stein companion and secretary really does have a legitimate connection to the cannabis-infused treats—though when you get down to it, they're not brownies at all; they're hand-rolled, vaguely health food–esque nuggets of confection with a Middle Eastern spice flair.

. . . .

As the story goes, Toklas, while being a vital part of the arts scene, wasn't necessarily the writer in the family—her "autobiography" was written by her lifelong companion, Gertrude Stein, for instance—and when it came time to hand in the manuscript for her popular autobiographical cookbook, *The Alice B. Toklas Cookbook* in the 1950s, many of the stories and recipes from her book were actually contributed by her bohemian buddies.

One of the artists she hit up was Brion Gysin, a sort of avant-garde Renaissance man who worked as a painter, writer, performance artist, and "sound poet." Followers of the Beat movement may recognize him as the inventor of the "dream machine," made famous when written about by William S. Burroughs. So why ask him for a recipe? Turns out, among his other talents he had been a restaurateur in Tangiers for a time. This was Gysin's entrée into Tangiers society and culture, including some of its many hallucinatory delights.

The restaurant went out of business after a few years, and Gysin went to live in Paris, taking lodgings in a flophouse that would later become famous as the Beat Hotel. It was in Paris that he became one of Alice B. Toklas and Gertrude Stein's pets.

Of course, he hadn't forgotten those delightful Moroccan discoveries, and when asked to produce a recipe, his entry was for something called Hashish Fudge. In the book, it's described as "easy to whip up on a rainy day" but warns that moderation is key and that one should be prepared for an onslaught of visions and thoughts on "many simultaneous planes."

Toklas claimed ignorance regarding the secret ingredient, later protesting that she didn't recognize the Latin name.

Needless to say, the readers noticed this subversive sweet right away, and it caused quite an uproar. While it was too late to remove the recipe from the UK printings, it was edited for the US release. For her part, Toklas claimed ignorance regarding the secret ingredient, later protesting that she didn't recognize the Latin name. Still, you can't un-ring a bell like that, and the naughty recipe was apparently great PR: the book went on to become a best-seller, and is considered a classic in the biographical cookbook genre.

Toklas's name became associated with not only the brownies, but with cannabis-infused foods of all sorts. The pop culture connection was sealed with the 1968 film *I Love You Alice B. Toklas*, in which a character portrayed by Peter Sellers leaves behind his boring life after falling in love with a pot brownie–baking free spirit. He goes on to become disenchanted with the hippie culture—but that's another story.

Toklas "Truffles"

THIS RECIPE MAKES MORSELS THAT ARE QUITE PLEASANT: dense with dried fruits and chopped nuts, not too sweet, and fragrant with distinctively Middle Eastern spices. Here's a "toke-less" recipe adapted from the famous one, because as the recipe itself notes, "Obtaining the cannabis may present certain difficulties . . ."

Makes 20 truffles

1½ teaspoons ground black peppercorns

½ teaspoon freshly ground nutmeg

½ teaspoon freshly ground cinnamon

1 teaspoon ground coriander

¼ cup dates

¼ cup dried figs

¼ cup almonds

¼ cup pistachios

1 cup packed dark brown sugar

3 tablespoons butter

1. Mix the peppercorns, nutmeg, cinnamon, and coriander together in a small bowl. Set aside.

2. Chop the dates, figs, almonds, and pistachios very finely; stir them together in a medium bowl. If you're including the special ingredient, now is when you'd add it. Just saying. Mix in the spices. Set aside.

3. In a medium saucepan over medium heat, melt the butter. Add the brown sugar and stir until it has mostly dissolved into the butter. Take the pan off the heat; add the rest of the ingredients and stir until the mixture comes together.

4. Roll the confections into small balls, or press the whole amount into a lightly buttered pan. Let set for about 30 minutes, or until it cools to room temperature. If you've pressed the mixture into a pan, cut it into small pieces before serving.

Better than Sex Cake

IT WOULD BE HIGHLY APPROPRIATE to place cakes in the category of pleasures such as pizza and sex, in that even when they're bad, they're *still good*. Still, there's a definite difference between good and so-bad-it's-good. And in the case of Better than Sex Cake, we're definitely into the latter territory.

· · · · · · · · · · · · · · · · · ·

There's a magnum-sized spectrum of varieties of this cake, but in its purest form it's comprised of cake mix, crushed pineapple, vanilla pudding mix, whipped topping, pecans, coconut, and—if you're lucky—a cherry on top. Though foodies may balk at this stellar cast of bad-decision ingredients, it's really quite tasty. If you want to get kinky, it even has an evil twin—one that features chocolate cake, caramel, sweetened condensed milk, crushed candy bars, and once again, whipped topping. Both versions are characterized by the method in the making, which includes poking the cake with the tines of a fork so the fillings can seep in, making for a cake that is somewhere between a trashy *tres leches* cake and a souped-up pudding cake.

It's a cake that has, over the years, been called other things: Almost Better than Sex Cake, Better than Robert Redford Cake, Finger Lickin' Good Cake, Earthquake Cake, Holy Cow Cake, OMG Cake. So why would it still be best known as the Better than Sex Cake? Probably for the same reason that Sex on the Beach is a cocktail favored at bachelorette parties over, say, a gin and tonic: it's far naughtier and more fun to say.

The originators of the cake are hard to pinpoint, as it seems to have taken off as a home-baked phenomenon, primarily in the 1970s. But—and this is important—it does seem to be closely connected to the invention of Cool Whip, that presweetened science experiment of a dessert topping, in 1967.

It's been a political cake, too: there's an amusing tale I heard from the *Charlotte Observer's* associate editor Jack Betts about Michigan politician

Though foodies may balk at this stellar cast of bad-decision ingredients, it's really quite tasty.

Ruth Easterling, a tiny powerhouse of a woman who always left an impression on people. Apparently, at a House Rules Committee meeting, one of the other politician's wives had brought a tempting cake, to which a seventy-something-year-old Easterling replied, "Well, I make a pretty good cake too . . . it's called Better than Sex Cake." Upon the response that a cake must be great with a name like that, live-wire Easterling shot right back, "It's not *that* good."

No, the feisty little old lady didn't invent the cake. But it's stories like these, along with the titter-inducing name, that have kept this recipe going. Perhaps the best summation of the cake comes in a hilarious 1990 article by humorist Erma Bombeck who, after having read about the cake, made it and—scandal!—served it to her kids. But instead of moaning and saying "Yes! Yes!" as the writer fantasizes, they sum it up rather matter of factly: "Mom, it's just a cake. You understand that, don't you?"

My recipe uses real whipped cream rather than the chemical-laden topping called for in many early recipes. Also, while the recipe calls for cake mix, you can substitute a cake made from scratch; Yellow Birthday Cake (page 5), works beautifully—but remember to increase the baking time by about five minutes, as the pan size is different.

Better than Sex Cake

THIS GUILTY-PLEASURE DESSERT WILL definitely leave you with equal parts regret and satiation (and even better: this recipe uses real whipped cream rather than the chemical-laden whipped topping called for in many recipes).

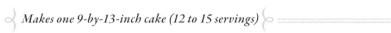

Makes one 9-by-13-inch cake (12 to 15 servings)

One 18.25-ounce package yellow cake mix

One 20-ounce can crushed pineapple with juice

¾ cup light brown sugar

One 5.1 ounce packages instant vanilla pudding mix

3 cups whole or 2% milk

1 cup heavy cream

¼ cup confectioners' sugar

1 teaspoon vanilla extract

¾ cup flaked coconut

½ cup chopped pecans

1. Bake the yellow cake according to the directions on the box for a 9-by-13-inch cake pan.

2. While the cake bakes, combine the pineapple (with its juice) and brown sugar in a medium saucepan. Cook over medium heat for about 20 minutes, stirring occasionally, until the liquid has reduced to the thickness of honey. Remove from the heat.

3. Once the cake has come out of the oven, place the pan on a wire rack. Do not remove the cake from the pan. Pierce the top of the still-hot cake with the tines of a fork at approximately 1-inch intervals. Pour the pineapple mixture over the cake. Spread it evenly, then let the cake cool completely.

4. In a medium bowl, whisk the pudding mix with the milk until smooth. Spread the pudding over the cake.

5. In the bowl of a stand mixer fitted with the whisk attachment, or using a large bowl with a hand whisk, whip the cream until slightly thickened. Add the confectioner's sugar and vanilla, then whip until soft peaks form. Spread over the top of the cake. Chill the cake for several hours or overnight to allow the flavors to meld.

6. To toast the coconut and pecans, preheat the oven to 300 degrees F. Spread the coconut evenly on a baking sheet and toast for about 5 minutes, until golden brown and crisp. Once or twice during the baking, toss the coconut so that it browns evenly. Then toast the pecans for 7 to 10 minutes, or until fragrant and lightly browned. Cool both at room temperature.

7. Just before serving, sprinkle the cake with the toasted coconut and pecans. Cover and refrigerate any leftovers; the cake will keep for about 3 days.

Katharine Hepburn Brownies

HERE IS A FANTASTIC AND TRUE STORY about Katharine Hepburn and her slightly cakey, slightly chewy, lightly chocolaty, nut-studded, and highly pleasant brownies. In the early 1980s, a Bryn Mawr student dropped a bombshell on her parents while home in New York City for the holidays: she was going to drop out of school, move to Scotland, and write screenplays. Needless to say, her father was the opposite of pleased. And so he did exactly what any worried parent would in such a situation: he wrote a letter to Katharine Hepburn, who had also attended Bryn Mawr, asking for help convincing his daughter to stay in school. "She's a great admirer of yours," he implored, "and perhaps she'll listen to you."

· · · · · · · · · · · · · · · · ·

As oddball a thing to do as this may seem, in this particular case it wasn't totally out of left field. As it turns out, this distraught father was a neighbor of Hepburn's, and would occasionally exchange pleasantries with her while, say, heading to the grocery store; let's say they were friendly acquaintances. And, well, desperate times call for desperate measures.

Upon receiving this cry for help, the imperious Hepburn didn't waste any time. She phoned at 7:30 the next morning, demanding to speak with the would-be dropout, who was sleeping at the time of the call but certainly awoke rapidly. Hepburn didn't mince words, admonishing, "What a damn stupid thing to do!" She then proceeded to deliver a stern lecture, after which she demanded that father and daughter come to tea at her home.

Upon arriving at Hepburn's nearby townhome on the date of the tea, the guests were greeted by Hepburn in her famously authoritative manner. She presented her guests with tea along with a plate of her famous brownies.

The recipe proved popular beyond a fad, and with good reason: these chewy brownies beautifully straddle the middle ground between cakey and fudgy brownies.

The brownies were already famous, of course. They had first surfaced in *Ladies' Home Journal* in 1975, accompanying an article by legendary gossip writer Liz Smith. The recipe appeared side by side an interview with Kate, who called them "the best brownies ever!" Where Hepburn got the recipe has always been vague, but no matter—the recipe was an instant hit, probably at first because the article provided an unexpected view into the life of the notoriously private Hepburn. But the recipe proved popular beyond a fad, and with good reason: these chewy brownies beautifully straddle the middle ground between cakey and fudgy brownies (perhaps tipping slightly more toward the fudge-like side).

But back to that young lady from Bryn Mawr. While there's no transcript of the tea party, let's just say the student remained at Bryn Mawr and went on to have a very successful career. While it might be a stretch to say the brownies themselves were responsible, certainly they made a sweet contribution to her story. This tale perfectly illustrates Hepburn's top three principles for a successful life, as chronicled by Liz Smith in her book *Dishing*: 1. Never quit; 2. Be yourself; 3. Don't put too much flour in your brownies.

Katharine Hepburn Brownies

ENJOY YOUR OWN TASTE OF SWEET SUCCESS with these easy-to-make brownies. They are in no way fussy, and the simple recipe yields fantastic results. And few brownies come with such a great story.

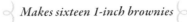

Makes sixteen 1-inch brownies

1. Preheat the oven to 325 degrees F. Grease the bottom and sides of an 8-inch square baking pan.

2. In a medium bowl, sift together the flour and salt. Set aside.

3. In a large saucepan over low heat, melt the chocolate and butter, stirring to make sure the chocolate doesn't stick or burn.

4. Once melted, remove from the heat and add the sugar, stirring until fully incorporated. Add the eggs and vanilla, beating by hand with a wooden spoon until fully incorporated.

5. Using a wooden spoon, stir in the flour mixture until fully incorporated. Fold in the walnuts.

6. Spoon the batter into your prepared baking pan. Bake for 35 to 40 minutes, or until a toothpick inserted into the center comes out mostly clean; it is better to err on slightly under—rather than overbaked—this will ensure a chewy texture.

7. Cool completely. Cut into 16 squares and serve.

¼ cup all-purpose flour

¼ teaspoon salt

2 ounces unsweetened chocolate, finely chopped (about ¼ cup)

½ cup (1 stick) unsalted butter, cut into small pieces, at room temperature

1 cup sugar

2 large eggs, lightly beaten

½ teaspoon vanilla extract

1 cup chopped, toasted walnuts (pecans or hazelnuts also work well)

Urban Legend Cookies

IT'S A LEGENDARY SORT OF COOKIE, dotted with two types of chocolate—morsels and grated—and packed full of nuts and oats. And like the cookie, the tale behind it is the stuff of gossip columns, a fine urban legend indeed. It's a Robin Hood tale of sorts, a cautionary tale of recipe rights.

. . . .

As the story goes (and there are many variations), a woman and her daughter are keeping up their energy while shopping at Neiman Marcus in Dallas, Texas, by snacking on a cookie in the luxe department store's café. Impressed, they ask for the recipe; they're informed that it will come with a "two-fifty" charge, which will be put on the mother's account. Not bad for a good recipe, right? But as it later turns out, the amount billed is $250, not a mere $2.50. Incensed, Mom photocopies the recipe and shares it with her friends, urging them to share it with *their* friends, so that the store will never make another penny off this cookie—and, more altruistically, so that its deliciousness might be enjoyed by all.

Well, as fun a story as it might be—the little guy giving "Needless Markup" the what-for—well, it's just not true. For one thing, it's a tale that has been circulated before: it's famously associated with the Waldorf Astoria hotel and their red velvet cake; also, a variation of the same cookie legend has been attached to Mrs. Fields cookies (much to their chagrin, I'm sure).

Here's the real clincher, though—before the emergence of this legend, the department store didn't sell their own chocolate chip cookies, much less have a recipe to share. But after the legend started circulating, you can bet your bottom dollar they got themselves a cookie recipe. Yes, indeed—they hired a recipe developer to create a cookie in response to the demand created by all the hubbub. Neiman Marcus has published the recipe in one of their cookbooks

After the legend started circulating, you can bet your bottom dollar they got themselves a cookie recipe. Yes, indeed—they hired a recipe developer to create a cookie in response to the demand created by all the hubbub.

(which, by the way, retails for less than $250) and has also shared it on their website.

With the advent of the Internet, the tale has also gone viral via an e-mail titled "Cookie Revenge."

That version of the recipe differs from the official Neiman Marcus cookie invented by the store: I, in homage to the Cookie Revenge movement, have created a lightly adapted version of the people's cookie. It yields a great cookie and a great number of them.

Urban Legend Cookies

IN ESSENCE, THIS RECIPE (which I guess I'll attribute to "the Internet") is an interesting riff on classic chocolate chip cookies—some would even say it's an improvement, based solely on the fact that it calls for both semisweet and milk chocolate. What appears to be an alarming amount of chocolate in this recipe actually doesn't come across as excessive in the final product, so fear not. You may just find yourself wanting to share it via chain letters . . . thus, continuing the legend.

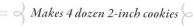 *Makes 4 dozen 2-inch cookies*

1. Preheat the oven to 375 degrees F. Line 3 baking sheets with parchment paper or reuse pans.

1. In a large bowl, stir together the flours, baking soda, baking powder, and salt. Set aside.

2. In the bowl of a stand mixer fitted with the paddle attachment, cream the butter and both sugars on medium-low speed until fluffy, 3 to 5 minutes.

3. Add the eggs, one at a time, pausing after each addition to scrape the sides of the bowl with a rubber spatula. Stir in the vanilla.

4. Add the flour mixture gradually, in 2 to 3 additions, scraping the sides of the bowl after each addition. Remove the bowl from the mixer and fold in the chocolate chips, grated chocolate, and nuts. Roll the dough into 1-inch balls and place them 2 inches apart on the prepared baking sheets.

5. Bake for 8 to 10 minutes, or until lightly browned. Let cool for a couple of minutes before transferring the cookies to a wire rack to cool completely.

6. Store the cookies at room temperature in an airtight container for up to 7 days, or store in the freezer for up to 1 month.

2½ cups oat flour (available at specialty food markets)

2 cups all-purpose flour, sifted

1 teaspoon baking soda

1 teaspoon baking powder

½ teaspoon salt

1 cup (2 sticks) unsalted butter, softened

1 cup granulated sugar

1 cup packed light brown sugar

2 large eggs

1 teaspoon vanilla extract

One 12-ounce bag (about 1½ cups) semisweet chocolate chips

6 ounces milk chocolate, grated (about 1 cup)

1½ cups chopped nuts (your choice)

SOURCES

WhatsCookingAmerica.net
ChowHound.com
FoodTimeline.org
American Food by Evan Jones
History of Baking in America Volumes I and II by
William G. Panschar
Rare Bits: Unusual Origins of Popular Recipes by
Patricia Bunning Stevens
Doughnuts: An American Passion by John T Edge
Betty Crocker's Cooky Book by Betty Crocker
Paris Sweets by Dorie Greenspan
A World of Cakes by Krystina Castella
A Baker's Odyssey by Greg Patent

BIRTHDAY CAKE (PAGE 3)
The Folk-lore Journal, Volume 1 and Volume 11
(accessible at http://en.wikisource.org/wiki/
Folk-Lore_Journal)
NewEnglandRecipes.org
RECIPE: I can't tell you where this recipe came
from—it's a basic cake that has been kicking
around in my repertoire forever, it seems. I've
been using it for my personal birthday cake for
years. The frosting is adapted from a version I
learned about from my friend Alice Currah, who
blogs at SavorySweetLife.com.

BOSTON CREAM PIE (PAGE 8)
Stern, Lisë. "Contest finalists and judges discover
the value of pie." *Boston Globe*, April 27, 2005
Omni Parker House Hotel
MALegislature.gov
You Know You're In Massachusetts When . . . by
Patricia Harris and David Lyon
RECIPE: Adapted from the original Omni Parker
House Hotel recipe.

BALLAD OF BETTY AND DUNCAN AND ALL MIXED UP SIDEBARS (PAGES 12, 43)
*Finding Betty Crocker: The Secret Life of America's
First Lady of Food* by Susan Marks
Bowling Green Area Convention &
Visitor's Bureau

CARROT CAKE (PAGE 13)
Oxford Companion to Food 2nd edition by Alan
Davidson
RECIPE: This recipe is an adaptation of a handwrit-
ten one I found in my friend Chris's repertoire.
I omitted the raisins (because I don't like them)
and added nuts.

CUPCAKES (PAGE 17)
American Cookery 1796 2nd edition by Amelia
Simmons
Scientific American magazine, September 2009
RECIPE: This is a coconut cake recipe that I changed
slightly to work in cupcake form. The frosting is
a coconutty adaptation of the version found in
my first book, *CakeSpy Presents Sweet Treats for a
Sugar-Filled Life.*

GERMAN CHOCOLATE CAKE (PAGE 22)
Baker's Chocolate (a division of Kraft Foods)
WhatsCookingAmerica.com
RECIPE: This is an adaptation of the version popularized as a back-of-the-box recipe. This version is
slightly more tender owing to cake flour, plus I've
upped the vanilla for a more flavorful end result
and topped it with a chocolate glaze.

NEW YORK CHEESECAKE (PAGE 26)
New York Times articles
*On Food And Cooking: The Science and Lore of the
Kitchen* by Harold McGee

RECIPE: This is an adaptation of a widely circulated recipe entitled "Lindy's Cheesecake," which I believe was first "outed" in the *New York Times* in the 1960s. Every version is a little different. This version is quite simple, but true to versions of that era.

DOUGHNUTS (PAGE 31)
Donuts: An American Passion by John T. Edge
A History of New York by Washington Irving
RECIPE: This recipe is based on one I photocopied from a women's magazine long ago (I'm sorry; I forget which one!). The original was a spiced doughnut recipe, but I prefer it plain. Through the years I have adjusted the proportions, so it is quite different from the original, and proof that one of the most joyous parts of a recipe is how it adapts over the years!

PINEAPPLE UPSIDE-DOWN CAKE (PAGE 35)
Dole Company
Hawaiian Pineapple as One Hundred Good Cooks Serve It (accessible at http://www.amazon.com/PINEAPPLE-contributed-magazine-reading-practical-Pineapple/dp/B003ATN3O8)
RECIPE: For this recipe, I consulted recipes both old and new. This is a sort of middle ground between them, with a cake that has an increased caramelly quotient thanks to brown sugar and an extra egg.

RED VELVET CAKE (PAGE 39)
Stella of BraveTart.com pointed me in many of the right directions for this one.
AdamsExtract.com
RECIPE: I started with a recipe I found a few years ago, but tinkered with the ratios and food-coloring amount. The boiled milk frosting is adapted from Warren Brown.

SMITH ISLAND CAKE (PAGE 45)
Mrs. Kitching's Smith Island Cookbook by Frances Kitching and Susan Stiles Dowell
RECIPE: Adapted from the recipe in *Mrs. Kitching's Smith Island Cookbook.*

BLONDIES & BROWNIES (PAGE 51)
FoodTimeline.org
The Encyclopedia of American Food & Drink by John F. Mariani
The Oxford Encyclopedia of Food and Drink in America, edited by Andrew F. Smith

CHOCOLATE CHIP COOKIES (PAGE 55)
The Wakefield Cookbook Collection, Framingham State University Library
New York Times articles
Ruth Wakefield's Toll House Tried and True Recipes by Ruth Graves Wakefield
Betty Crocker's Cooky Book by Betty Crocker
RECIPE: Adapted from the original Toll House recipe.

PEANUT BUTTER COOKIES (PAGE 58)
Claiborne, Craig. "The Fork and the Cookie." *New York Times*, April 2, 1979.
Schenectady Journal, 1932.
How to Grow the Peanut and 105 Ways of Preparing it for Human Consumption by George W. Carver
RECIPE: Adapted from the one my mom always made while I was growing up!

PUFFED RICE TREATS (PAGE 61)
Kellogg's company timeline (KelloggHistory.com/timeline.html)
Mildred Day obituary. *Baltimore Sun*, June 14, 1996.
RECIPE: Adapted from the original back-of-the-box recipe on Rice Krispies.

WHOOPIE PIES (PAGE 65)
New York Times articles
PaDutchCountry.com
Labadie's Bakery
RECIPE: Adapted from a recipe by Judith Fertig.

APPLE PIE (PAGE 68)

The American Century Cookbook: The Most Popular Recipes of the 20th Century by Jean Anderson

Food and Drink in Britain: From the Stone Age to the 19th Century by C. Anne Wilson

RECIPE: Adapted from a recipe from the 1912 *Boston Cooking-School Cook Book* by Fannie Merritt Farmer.

NUTTY CHOCOLATE PIE (PAGE 71)

Epicurious.com

Encyclopedia of Louisville by John E. Kleber

Pearl, Charlie. "Still Playing the Pie Game." *The State Journal*, April 17, 2008. http://www.state-journal.com/local%20news/2008/04/17/still-playing-the-pie-game

850 F.2d 692. United States Court of Appeals, Sixth Circuit. http://bulk.resource.org/courts.gov/c/F2/850/850.F2d.692.87-6152.87-5852.html

RECIPE: Adapted from a recipe for a race day pie in *Southern Living* (I believe).

LEMON MERINGUE PIE (PAGE 75)

Mrs. Goodfellow's Cookery As It Should Be by Mrs. Goodfellow

An A–Z of Food & Drink by John Ayto and Alan Davidson

HistoryCooks.com

RECIPE: Custard adapted from my mom; recipe is a mash-up of several classics.

PECAN PIE (PAGE 79)

Bok, Edward William and Louisa Knapp. *Ladies' Home Journal*, Volume 15

The Southern Cook Book of Fine Old Recipes by Lillie S. Lustig

The Cambridge World History of Food by Kenneth F. Kiple and Kriemhild Coneè Ornelas

PUMPKIN PIE (PAGE 83)

America's Founding Food: The Story of New England Cooking by Keith Stavely and Kathleen Fitzgerald

Eating in America by Waverley Root and Richard de Rochemont

RECIPE: Based on the famous back-of-the-label recipe from Libby's canned pumpkin.

BAKED ALASKA (PAGE 89)

WhatsCookingAmerica.com

FoodReference.com

The Glutton's Glossary: A Dictionary of Food and Drink Terms by John Ayto

RECIPE: The idea for the brownie base came from Catherine McCord of Weelicious.com

HERMITS (PAGE 93)

HistoryCook.com

NewEnglandRecipes.org

The American History Cookbook by Mark Zanger

Miss Parloa's New Cook Book 1880 edition by Maria Parloa

Betty Crocker's Cooky Book by Betty Crocker

RECIPE: Adapted and inspired by a combination of recipes found in *Miss Parloa's New Cook Book* and *Betty Crocker's Cooky Book*.

JOE FROGGERS (PAGE 95)

Weltner, Linda. "History of Black Joe." *Marblehead Magazine.*

New England Cookbook by Eleanor Early

Marblehead Myths, Legends and Lore by Pam Matthias Peterson

RECIPE: Adapted from the historical recipe found on the Marblehead website (Marblehead.org).

JUMBLES (PAGE 97)

Hearthside Cooking: Early American Southern Cuisine by Nancy Carter Crump

The Accomplisht Cook by Robert May

Betty Crocker's Cooky Book by Betty Crocker

Martha Washington's Booke of Cookery by Karen Hess

Mrs. Beeton's Every-Day Cookery by
  Mrs. Isabella Beeton
RECIPE: Adapted from Eliza Leslie.

TUNNEL OF FUDGE CAKE (PAGE 101)
Pillsbury archives
H. David Dalquist obituary. *New York Times*, 2005.
RECIPE: Pillsbury was generous enough to permit
  me to use this recipe.

WELLESLEY FUDGE CAKE (PAGE 105)
Wellesley College Staff
AmericasTestKitchen.com
Baker's Chocolate (a division of Kraft Foods)
RECIPE: Adapted from an early 1900s recipe which
  appeared on Baker's Chocolate boxes.

ANZAC BISCUITS (PAGE 110)
"Protection of Word 'Anzac' Regulations."
  Australian Government: Department of
  Verteran's Affairs. http://www.comlaw.gov.au/
  Series/F1997B02175
Fewster, Sean. "Subway dumps Anzac biscuit from
  the menu." *The Advertiser*, September 22, 2008.
RECIPE: Adapted from a recipe in *The Register New-
  Pictorial* in the 1930s.

CHERRIES JUBILEE (PAGE 113)
White Truffles in Winter by N. M. Kelby
Brennan's Restaurant
Hitchcock, Max. "Cherries Jubilee created
  for Queen Victoria." *The Citizen*, November
  30, 2005. http://auburnpub.com/lifestyles/
  article_115089e4-ab4a-5db7-b4ff-b367f1728cf4
  .html?print=1
RECIPE: Adapted from recipes by Paula Deen,
  Rachael Ray, and AllRecipes.com.

CROISSANTS (PAGE 116)
*August Zang and the French Croissant: How
  Viennoiserie Came to France* by Jim Chevallier
RECIPE: Adapted from a recipe by Jennifer Lee.

GINGERBREAD MEN (PAGE 121)
*The Christmas Cook: Three Centuries of American
  Yuletide Sweets* by William Woys Weaver
Edwards, Karen S. and Sharon Antle.
  "Gingerbread." *Americana* magazine.
"Holiday Tradition with Spicy History." *Pittsburgh
  Post-Gazette*, December 9, 2001.
RECIPE: Adapted from a Margie Moore original
  (that's my mom!).

OPERA CAKE (PAGE 125)
*Paris Sweets: Great Desserts From the City's Best
  Pastry Shops* by Dorie Greenspan
Larousse Gastronomique by Librairie Larousse
*La Nouvelle Patisserie: The Art and Science of
  Making Beautiful Pastries and Desserts* by Jean-
  Yves DuPerret and Jacqueline Mallorca
RECIPE: Adapted from a Dorie Greenspan recipe.

PRINCESS TORTE (PAGE 131)
*The Professional Pastry Chef: Fundamentals of
  Baking and Pastry* by Bo Friberg
Prinsessornas Kokbok by Jenny Akerstrom and
  Gudrun Carlson
SemiSwede.com
RECIPE: Adapted from original Jenny Akerstrom
  recipes and Greg Patent.

ANIMAL CRACKERS (PAGE 139)
Songs for a Little House by Christopher Morley
Leiby, Richard. "Send In The Clowns." *The
  Washington Post*, November 20, 2005. http://
  www.washingtonpost.com/wp-dyn/content/
  article/2005/11/19/AR2005111901467_pf.html
Extraordinary Origins of Everyday Things
  by Charles Panati
Sydney Stern obituary. *New York Times*, 1989.

RECIPE: Believe it or not, this was adapted from a recipe I received that was on the back-of-the-box of a box of cookie cutters that were gifted to me!

GIRL SCOUT COOKIES (PAGE 143)
GirlScouts.org
RECIPE: Adapted from an early Girl Scout cookie recipe.

CHOCOLATE CREME-FILLED COOKIES (PAGE 147)
Kraft Foods, INC 100 Years of Oreo Fact Sheet
Out of the Cracker Barrel: From Animal Crackers to ZuZu's by William Cahn
Rhoads, Christopher. "Hydrox Redux: Cookie Duels Orea, Again." *The Wall Street Journal*, May 28, 2008.
RECIPE: Originally published in *Retro Desserts* by Wayne Harley Brachman, this recipe was adopted and adapted online quite a bit. I followed several of the adaptations and made my own. It is quite different from the "original" recipe at this point!

PINK FROSTED COOKIES (PAGE 151)
PinksOriginalBakery.com
RECIPE: This recipe is a basic softie sugar cookie with pink frosting. It's not meant to be a copy of the pink frosted cookie, which is rolled; this one is much easier for the home baker with a tight schedule!

TOASTER-STYLE PASTRIES (PAGE 156)
Barry, Dave. "Tarts Afire." The *Herald*, June 27, 1993.
Kellogg's company timeline (KelloggHistory.com/timeline.html)
Whole Pop online magazine (WholePop.com)
RECIPE: This is similar to the one that appeared in my first book, *CakeSpy Presents Sweet Treats for a Sugar-Filled Life* (which was adapted from a recipe by Peabody Rudd) with slight edits.

ALICE B. TOKLAS BROWNIES (PAGE 160)
The Alice B. Toklas Cookbook by Alice B. Toklas
"Alice B. Toklas Life Stories, Books, & Links." *Today in Literature*. www.todayinliterature.com/biography/alice.b.toklas.asp
Nothing Is True—Everything Is Permitted: The Life of Brion Gysin by John Geiger
RECIPE: This is adapted from the original in *The Alice B. Toklas Cookbook*, but designed for a more modern audience and with the option to make as bars or as truffles.

BETTER THAN SEX CAKE (PAGE 163)
Bombeck, Erma. "Cake Dubbed Better than Sex." *Ocala Star-Banner*, Oct 30, 1990.
Amusing anecdote from Jack Betts of *The Charlotte Observer*
RECIPE: Starting on the Internet, I found many versions of this recipe. I have combined various aspects of several for this version.

KATHARINE HEPBURN BROWNIES (PAGE 167)
"Straight Talk from Miss Hepburn" letter to the editor. *New York Times*, July 6, 2003.
Dishing: Great Dish—and Dishes—from America's Most Beloved Gossip Coumnist by Liz Smith
Ladies' Home Journal magazine
RECIPE: This recipe has been widely shared. This is a little bit more informative version of it.

URBAN LEGEND COOKIES (PAGE 171)
BreakTheChain.org
Neiman Marcus
RECIPE: Adapted from various recipes around the Internet; this is *not* the one that Neiman Marcus started selling!

INDEX

Note: Photographs are indicated by *italics*.

ABOUT THE AUTHOR

JESSIE OLESON MOORE is a triple threat: writer/illustrator/baker. After attending Pratt Institute in Brooklyn and working at two stationery companies, she branched off to start her own business. A self-described "seeker of sweetness in everyday life," she reports on her sweet findings, sharing recipes and illustrations of desserts on her popular website CakeSpy.com. Apparently afflicted with wanderlust, she has recently lived in Seattle, Philadelphia, and New York City.